book indexing
a step-by-step guide

book indexing

a step-by-step guide

Stephen Ullstrom

Copyright © 2023 Stephen Ullstrom
All rights reserved

All rights reserved under international copyright conventions. No part of this publication may be reproduced, stored in or introduced into a retrieval system, or transmitted in any form or by any means, without the prior written permission of the author.

First edition

ISBN 978-1-7388250-0-4 (paperback)
ISBN 978-1-7388250-1-1 (eBook)
ISBN 978-1-7388250-2-8 (PDF)

Editing by Mary Newberry
Copyediting by Alexandra Peace
Cover and interior design by David W. Edelstein
Index by Jolanta Komornicka

Anthimus Press
Edmonton, AB, Canada
www.stephenullstrom.com

For everyone who loves and appreciates an excellent index

Contents

Preface xi
    Why I Wrote This Book xi
    Who This Book Is For xi
    Terminology xii

1. Should You Write Your Own Index? 1
    What Is an Index? 1
    What Is Not an Index? 2
    The Mystery of the Well-Written Index 3
    Does Your Book Need an Index? 8
    One Index or Multiple? 8
    Should You Write Your Own Index? 9
    How to Use This Guide 10
    Takeaways 12
    Try This 13

2. The Basic Components 15
    Entries 15
    Arrays 16
    Main Headings 16
    Subheadings 17
    Locators 20
    Cross-References 22
    Takeaways 25
    Try This 26

3. Term Selection: What is Your Book About? 27
    Audience: Who is the Index for? 27
    Aboutness and the Hierarchy of Information 29

    Metatopic 31
    Supermain Discussions and Headings 33
    Regular Discussions and Headings 33
    All the Little Bits 34
    Significant Insignificant Details 35
    Passing Mentions 36
    Building a House 38
    Takeaways 38
    Try This 39

4. Structure: Putting the Pieces Together 41
    Building from the Table of Contents 41
    When the Structure Is Less Clear 47
    Multiple Access Points 58
    Takeaways 61
    Try This 61

5. Format: Laying the Ground Rules 63
    Layout 64
    Sub-Subheadings 67
    Em-dash-modified Format 72
    Sorting 81
    Numbers and Symbols 90
    Capitalization 90
    Takeaways 91
    Try This 93

6. Five-Step Framework for Indexing 95
    Step 1: Get Ready 96
    Step 2: Read the Text 98
    Step 3: Write the Rough Draft 102
    Step 4: Edit the Index 106
    Step 5: Solicit Feedback 108
    Layout and Typesetting 109
    Indexing from a List of Terms 110

Updating an Index 112
My Indexing Process 114
Takeaways 115
Try This 116

7. The Finer Points of Indexing 119

Consistency 119
Comprehensiveness 120
Headnotes and Explanatory Notes 122
Undifferentiated and Unruly Locators 123
Footnotes and Endnotes 128
Wording 130
Jargon, Terms of Art, and Plain Language 132
Neutral language 134
Offensive Language 137
Names 138
Glosses 139
Art, Books, Films, Music, Newspapers, and Other Creative Works 143
Triage for Space Constraints 146
Takeaways 150
Try This 151

8. Tips for Indexing Different Types of Books 153

Trade versus Scholarly 154
Monographs versus Edited Collections 155
History 156
Biography, Memoir, and Family History 157
Letters and Journals 161
How-To and Self-Help 162
Business Books 164
Guidebooks 164
Children's Books 166
Cookbooks 167
Health and Medical Books 169

Legal Books 170
Name Indexes 170
Index Locorum and Scripture Indexes 171
Fiction and Fictional Characters 174
Policies and Procedures, Reports, and User Manuals 177
Takeaways 178
Try This 179

9. Go Forth and Index **181**

Becoming a Professional Indexer 181
Training to Be an Indexer 183
Hiring an Indexer 184
Software for Indexing 186
EBook Indexes and Embedded Indexing 187

Acknowledgments **189**

Resources **191**

Glossary 191
Books, Articles, and Other Resources 195
Indexing Societies 200

Bibliography of Examples **203**

Index **207**

Preface

WHY I WROTE THIS BOOK

WRITING AN INDEX IS HARD. I do not want to sugarcoat this fact.

Indexing is a completely different skill set from writing or editing. Indexing is about deconstructing a book into its components and reassembling all that information into an easily searchable format. While understanding what the book is about is important, so is understanding all the rules and conventions that govern indexes.

Indexing is also a skill that can be taught. That is why I have written this book.

This book is intended as a practical introduction to indexing. In the first several chapters, I cover the basic principles and techniques and provide step-by-step guidance to help you quickly get started. I explore indexing in greater detail in later chapters. My intention is to make indexing accessible and to help you avoid pitfalls so that you can more quickly and easily write an excellent index.

WHO THIS BOOK IS FOR

This book is for anyone interested in learning about book indexing, from authors thinking about indexing their own book to people considering indexing as a career.

My original reason for writing this book was to help authors write better indexes. Some authors write their own indexes, whether out of curiosity, because they enjoy the process, or because hiring a professional is too expensive. I also admire authors who index their own books, because that speaks to how much the author values an index, and I know that indexing is not easy. This book is an offering, to help demystify and simplify the process.

I am also aware of people considering indexing as a career and wanting to learn more. This book is for you as well. While there are other books aimed at professional indexers, I have tried to make this book a thorough introduction, covering all the basics in a way that is easy to read and providing practical guidance on how to write and complete an index.

Whatever your motivation for reading this book, thank you for valuing indexes enough to learn more. I look forward to walking with you through the indexing process.

TERMINOLOGY

Indexing, as with many specialized subjects, has its own jargon. I try to briefly define terms in the text as I use them. There is also a glossary at the end of the book, on page 191.

Please note that while some terms, such as subheadings and locators, are commonly accepted across the indexing world, indexers have less agreement on the definitions of other terms, such as arrays and entries. Defining terms for this book inevitably requires me to stake out my own position, knowing that some respected colleagues would beg to differ. My goal is to keep terminology as clear and simple as possible. I will also do my best to point out synonymous terms and alternative definitions, which you may encounter in other resources.

1

Should You Write Your Own Index?

WHAT IS AN INDEX?

AN INDEX IS A DOCUMENT created to help users access information. In this book, I will focus on writing indexes for books, but indexes can also be written for other repositories of information, such as journals, magazines, and newspapers; databases; and websites.

The *Canadian Oxford Dictionary, Second Edition* defines an index as, "an alphabetical list of names, subjects, etc. with references, usually at the end of a book." *Merriam-Webster* concurs, stating, "a list of items (such as topics or names) treated in a printed work that gives for each item the page number where it may be found." These definitions describe the format of an index—in list form, usually alphabetical—and state that indexes typically include topics and names, along with directions, through page numbers or other references, to where more information can be found.

Let's add a few more elements to flesh out what transforms a mediocre index into a quality index.

An index

- has a structure that aids navigation,
- presents information in small, easily digestible chunks, and

- accurately represents the contents of the book, while also anticipating the needs of the audience.

Writing an index requires the indexer to both understand the original text and make conscious decisions about how to present that information to readers. While there is software that promises to extract and list words found in the text, there is so far no substitute to a human's ability to reason and synthesize.

WHAT IS NOT AN INDEX?

Concordances

The index is often confused with a concordance. The concordance is also an alphabetical list of important terms that point to specific locations in the original text. The difference is that a concordance is simply a list. Sometimes decisions are made about which terms to include (but sometimes not!), and deeper analysis is not provided. Relationships between terms are not provided, larger discussions are not broken down using subheadings, and implicit discussions are not picked up. For example, the concordance may include arrays for barley, rye, and wheat, but the underlying concepts of agriculture, food, or grains may be omitted because those terms are not explicitly used. In addition, no connection is made between the three grains.

Table of Contents

An index is also different from a table of contents. Some books, including this one, have an extensive table of contents, listing section headings in addition to chapter titles. While the table of contents can be a useful finding aid, allowing readers to scan for the chapter or section that they desire, it is not a replacement for an index. The table of contents is a big-picture approach, leaving out details too small to warrant a chapter or section. The table of contents is also organized by page order, potentially a barrier to quickly pinpointing information, compared to the alphabetical order used in the index. Lastly, to be most useful, the chapter titles and section headers need to be clearly written, which is not always true. Some books—following genre conventions, to make a dry subject more lively, or to reflect the author's voice—use imaginative and playful language that, while fun and appropriate for that context, is not always clear.

Keyword Search

Indexes are also different from keyword search. This is what people often use in search engines or electronic documents like ebooks or PDFs. As a finding aid, keyword search has three main problems. The first is relevance. All hits will appear, whether five or fifty, in an undifferentiated list, and it is the user's responsibility to determine which of them, if any, are relevant. A well-written index, on the other hand, will do that sorting on behalf of the user, weeding out irrelevant hits and sorting what remains into a searchable format.

The second issue is that keyword search will often only find exact matches. Search will not find misspelled words, alternative conjugations, or implicit discussions. Locating names can be tricky, as a person may be referred to by a partial name, a pronoun, or title. An index, however, brings all these references together, and the user does not have to worry about missing hits due to an inexact search.

The last issue is that unexpected discovery is much more difficult with keyword search. There are either hits or no hits, whereas an index is browsable. The list of terms has already been created, and the reader can, if they wish, scan entries and make serendipitous discoveries.

THE MYSTERY OF THE WELL-WRITTEN INDEX

Writing an index is also about making decisions. Hundreds and thousands of decisions. Some of these decisions may be made by the publisher, such as decisions about format and length, while other decisions, such as what entries to include and how to structure the index, you will need to make yourself.

Let's look at an index and see how this decision making can play out. The following is a short autobiographical index that I wrote, both to introduce myself and to introduce how indexes function. It only contains thirty-nine entries, but I still spent time going back and forth on the best way to put it together.

A
awards, indexing
    Ewart-Daveluy Indexing Award, 21
    Purple Pen Award, 14

C
Canadian Literature (journal), 8–9

E
Ewart-Daveluy Indexing Award, 21

H
Harbour Publishing, 11–12

I
indexing
    awards won, 14, 21
    first index, 11
    started freelancing, 12
    training from SFU, 12
Indexing Society of Canada/Société canadienne d'indexation (ISC/SCI)
    Ewart-Daveluy Indexing Award, 21
    on executive committee, 15–16
    first joined, 12
    mentorship program, 18–19
Institute of Certified Indexers
    Purple Pen Award, 14

P
Purple Pen Award, 14

S
Simon Fraser University (SFU) indexing course, 12

T
Taiwan
    arrival as toddler, 2
    departure after high school graduation, 4
    last visit home, 19–20
tree planting, 5, 6

U
UBC Press, 11
Ullstrom, Stephen
    birth, 1
    at *Canadian Literature*, UBC Press, and Harbour Publishing, 8–9, 11–12
    childhood in Taiwan, 2–4
    chrismation into Orthodox Church, 8
    first index, 11
    marriage to Elim, 15
    started freelancing business, 12
    tree planting, 5, 6
    undergraduate at UBC, 5–7
    See also awards, indexing; indexing; Indexing Society of Canada/Société canadienne d'indexation (ISC/SCI); Taiwan
University of British Columbia (UBC), 5–7

In my discussion below, key indexing terms are in bold, to show how these concepts appear in this index.

As I mentioned, this autobiographical index contains thirty-nine **entries**. An entry is a single unit, composed of a **main heading**, possibly one or more levels of **subheadings**, and one **locator**. "Harbour Publishing, 11–12" is a single entry, with a main heading and locator. "Taiwan: arrival as toddler, 2," is also an entry, with the addition of a subheading. An entry directs the reader to a single place.

This index is also composed of fourteen **arrays**, also known as entry arrays. An array is a complete unit, containing everything that the index has to say about the subject. An array can be a single entry, as in "UBC Press, 11," or an array can be composed of multiple entries. The largest array in this index is for "Ullstrom, Stephen."

Structure is one of the more challenging aspects of indexing. A good index is well-organized, yet it can be difficult to sort and make sense of so many entries. A lot of time can be spent figuring out where to best place entries and arrays.

The **metatopic** of this index—what the index as a whole is about—is me. Since everything in this index is a potential subheading under my name, and since readers may first search for my name, "Ullstrom, Stephen" is the largest array.

However, there are aspects of my life that are important in their own right, and some readers may only be interested in these specific areas. So, I have also created separate arrays, for "awards, indexing," "indexing," "Indexing Society of Canada/Société canadienne d'indexation (ISC/SCI)," and "Taiwan," which also have subheadings, detailing those specific areas of my life and career. These are the **supermain headings** and **regular headings**, corresponding to **supermain discussions** and **regular discussions**. Users of this index now have options for how broadly or narrowly they would like to search. This is one way to provide **multiple access points**.

I have also chosen to **double-post**, or even triple-post, certain entries, which is another way to provide multiple access points. The Ewart-Daveluy Indexing Award, for example, is a standalone array as well as a subheading under "awards, indexing" and "Indexing Society of Canada/Société canadienne d'indexation (ISC/SCI)."

When double-posting, however, I have not always used identical wording, and I have at times chosen to conflate entries within subheadings. Each array is unique, and it is important to phrase the subheadings in a way that makes sense in relation to that particular main heading. For example, I have a standalone array for the University of British Columbia, which I have contextualized in a subheading under "Ullstrom, Stephen" as "undergraduate at UBC." I have also taken the three separate arrays for *Canadian Literature*, UBC Press, and Harbour Publishing—my three publishing jobs prior to freelancing—and combined them into a single subheading under "Ullstrom, Stephen," rather than treating them as separate subheadings. For the *Canadian Literature* array, I also decided to clarify, using a **gloss**, that *Canadian Literature* is a journal.

I have also chosen to not double-post everything under "Ullstrom, Stephen." I see that array as an overview of my life—personal, professional, and education—but for more specific details about my career readers will need to search under "indexing" and "Indexing Society of Canada/Société canadienne d'indexation (ISC/SCI)." For example, I only mention being on the ISC/SCI executive committee and first joining the society under the ISC/SCI array. Instead of double-posting, I have used **cross-references** from "Ullstrom, Stephen" to redirect readers to where they can find more information.

One of the trickier decisions I faced was what to use for **locators**. Locators are the element in the index that tells readers where to go for more information. Cross-references are a form of locator, directing readers to another place within the index. But most locators direct readers outside the index, to whatever is being indexed, usually a book or other document. When indexing a book, page numbers are usually used. My challenge, for this autobiographical index, is that there is no book or article about my life. For the sake of this example, I decided to use fictional page numbers, though I also considered using something more abstract, like dates (such as 2004 and 2011–2012), which do not point towards a text but instead reveal when events happened.

Decisions have consequences. Using dates instead of page numbers would have led to a different user experience. My choice of structure, with a metatopic array and supermain and regular arrays, informed where I placed and double-posted certain subheadings. While this index includes both professional and personal details, I still chose what to include and what to exclude.

Indexes are deceptively simple. They are written as a list, and everyone knows how a list functions. But under the surface are countless decisions. Making the index appear effortless—and making the index easy for readers to use—requires work. That is what I am going to teach you.

DOES YOUR BOOK NEED AN INDEX?

Chances are, yes, your book needs an index.

An index is a powerful finding tool, which is difficult to replace with other search methods.

Think about your book's purpose. If the book advances an argument, is intended to teach, or to serve as a resource, then a well-written index will enhance the ability of readers to access the information contained within.

Also consider the expectations of your audience and how your readers will use the book. Will readers use the book for research or as a resource? Will they read the book from cover to cover or will they dip in and out as needed? Or are readers primarily expecting to be entertained? An index can also serve as a marketing tool: some readers prefer to buy books with indexes, and some readers may also browse the index prior to buying, to see if the book contains relevant information.

It is also important to consider the purpose of the index itself. What is it about the book that you want the index to convey? Is it recipes? Hiking trails and parks? People and resources? Important concepts within the discipline? A general index containing all the above? A clear vision for the index, combining what the book is about with what readers will want to search for, will help guide you through the indexing process.

It is true that not all books require an index. Some books are written purely for fun, or for an audience that is happy without. Take a moment to think through your book and your reasons for indexing. Make sure that the index will add value for the intended audience.

ONE INDEX OR MULTIPLE?

Once you have decided to write an index, how many indexes does the book need?

Generally speaking, one is enough. Most indexes mix all entries together, regardless of the subject or type of entry. This makes it easy for the reader, as the reader only needs to search in one place.

Sometimes, though, multiple indexes are helpful and may even be expected in certain disciplines. In biblical and theological studies, for example, it is common to have a separate scripture index, listing all scripture references, in addition to the general index for subjects and names. In other disciplines, like psychology, separate name and subject indexes might be required.

Another reason to write multiple indexes is if there are only two or three elements that you wish to pick up. In this instance, the multiple indexes act as a filter, telling readers upfront that these are the only types of information available for searching. I did this for *Hunters on the Track: William Penny and the Search for Franklin*, by W. Gillies Ross. The budget for indexing was tight, and so the publisher and I decided on three indexes, for people, places, and ships. Anything which was not a person, place, or ship was not indexed. For other books, there may only be two or three indexable elements. For *Exploring the Capital: An Architectural Guide to the Ottawa-Gatineau Region*, by Andrew Waldron, I wrote one index for buildings and another for names, which included architects, architectural firms, and other people. The two indexes neatly summarized what the book was about, and gave readers two options for how to search.

If you are not sure how many indexes to include, check with your publisher or review similar books in the field to see what others have done. Also consider what you want the index to convey. If a wide variety of entries, then a single index is best. If a specific type of information needs to be highlighted, then two or more indexes may be justified.

SHOULD YOU WRITE YOUR OWN INDEX?

This is the crux of the matter.

Indexing is hard work and will require an investment of time. Depending on how long your book is, and how much time you can dedicate per day, you will probably need at least a week, possibly a month, to write an index.

Indexing is also much easier if you find it an interesting, engaging process. Do you delight in puzzles? In creating order out of chaos? In paying attention to detail? If indexing instead sounds tedious, then it may not be for you.

Financial cost is also a factor, as hiring a professional can be expensive, especially if you are paying out of pocket. Writing the index yourself will save money.

You may also be interested in indexing as a career or be curious and want to give it a try. These are also valid reasons for writing an index.

Many professional indexers emphasize that indexing is a specialized skill that requires training and practice to do well. Their recommendation is to hire a professional.

Being a professional indexer myself, I am sympathetic to that perspective. I also believe that indexing is a skill that can be taught; and I understand that not everyone wants to or is able to hire a professional. If you want to create an index, I believe that you can do it.

As you decide, consider the costs. This includes both time and money, which can be saved or spent. Also think about your personal interest in indexing. If indexing sounds like drudgery, hiring someone will save you a lot of angst and frustration.

If you decide, after all, to hire a professional, I provide some tips on page 184 for finding and working with an indexer. If you want to write your own index, read on!

HOW TO USE THIS GUIDE

This book is intended to walk you through the indexing process and to explain how an index works. You can either read this book and work through the exercises while writing an index, or you can read the book and write an index later.

Chapter 1 discusses what an index is and whether you should write your own. Chapter 2 digs deeper into the basic components of an index, while chapter 3 discusses how information is structured in a book and

How Much Time Does Indexing Require?

For a two-hundred-page book, plan to spend at least twenty to forty hours writing the index.

One of the main variables is how complicated the text is. Trade books, for a general audience, are often quicker to index, while scholarly books, for an academic audience, are often more difficult. Book size also plays a factor, with shorter books generally having less material to pick up and longer books having a lot more information to juggle.

If you are new to indexing, also factor in time for learning this new skill.

The other main factor is that indexing requires significant intellectual labor. It is not easy maintaining focus for hours on end, and decision-making fatigue can be a real problem. Among indexers I know, productivity typically falls off after about four to six hours of work per day. A marathon indexing session over the weekend is not realistic.

I recommend breaking the work up into smaller chunks and spreading the work over at least a week. When writing the rough draft, aim for indexing a chapter or two a day, depending on how long the chapters are, or to index a certain number of pages a day. When you begin indexing, first see what feels like a comfortable pace, and then plan how to tackle the rest of the book.

Similarly, break editing the index into two or more days. It can take more time than anticipated. I also find that the indexing process works best if I can give myself some distance from the work, for my subconscious to process the work and to see the index with fresh eyes.

If you do only have a weekend or two, or need to write the index within a few days, still try to break the work up into smaller chunks, rather than working continuously. Work two to four hours in the morning, take a break for a few hours, and then put in another session in the afternoon or evening. Your brain will appreciate the rest.

how to use that hierarchy of information to select terms for the index. Chapter 4 discusses how the hierarchy of information can also be used to develop the index's structure, and chapter 5 explores format.

With the groundwork laid for understanding how an index functions, chapter 6 lays out a simple five-step process for writing an index. Chapter 7 continues that discussion by considering ways to fine-tune your index, while chapter 8 provides tips on indexing different types of books. The book concludes with more information should you want to hire an indexer or explore indexing as a career.

Each chapter concludes with a short set of takeaways, along with a Try This section, containing exercises and tips for learning the material and moving forward with your own index.

If you are short on time, you can skip ahead to chapter 6 to learn the basic indexing process. You can also skim the rest of the chapters (or the index) to see if there is anything relevant for your particular index, and you can always come back to this book for answers if questions arise while indexing.

Note that in this book I follow North American usage, which is primarily based on the *Chicago Manual of Style*. Basic indexing techniques and practices are fairly universal, while specific formatting conventions and other practices may vary in other parts of the world. If you are working with a publisher, always check for their expectations and specifications.

TAKEAWAYS

- An index is a tool for helping readers find information in the text. It is more robust than other finding aids, such as concordances, tables of contents, and keyword search, and is best written by humans who both understand the original text and the needs of the audience.

- At its core, writing an index is a process of making decisions. The goal is to write an index that is easy for users to navigate and that enables users to quickly find information.

- Most nonfiction books are written to convey information. A well-written index makes that information much more accessible.

- A single index, covering both subject matter and names, is usually sufficient and is a solid default option. Sometimes, though, multiple indexes are better, depending on the needs of the audience or the types of information needing to be indexed.

- Indexing takes time, and requires significant intellectual labor. Make sure to schedule the appropriate time.

TRY THIS

- Write your own autobiographical index. It does not need to be long. Treat this as an exercise to reflect on indexing as a series of decisions. What information will you include about your life? How will you organize the information? What will you use for locators? How do different decisions either constrain or create new possibilities?

- If you are preparing to write an index, think about why. Also consider the costs—time, money, focus—that you would either be saving or spending. Is this something you want to do or are willing to do, or would it be better to find someone else?

- Writing an index takes time. Begin thinking about when you will make time to index and how you might break the work into smaller chunks. If you do not know, find out if there is a deadline for completing the index. Once you begin indexing, you can always adjust this schedule as needed.

- Think about what information needs to be included in your index. Is one index better, or multiple indexes? What will better serve the readers? Does the publisher have a preference? How do similar books handle the index?

- In preparation for exercises later in this book, pick a handful of books with indexes that you can examine and refer to. A good way to learn about indexing is to compare existing indexes and see how they measure up to best practices. For now, just select a few books and keep them handy. They can be from your own bookshelves or found online (Amazon's Look Inside feature will often allow you to see the index). If you are preparing to index a book, it may be helpful for at least one of these books to be on a similar topic or in the same genre. As you learn more about indexes, you may also discover that none of these books have a good index. You are welcome to add more books to this pile as you learn and desire better examples.

2

The Basic Components

EVERY INDEX IS COMPOSED OF the same basic components. They are:

- entries
- arrays
- main headings
- subheadings
- locators
- cross-references

ENTRIES

The entry is the smallest unit in the index. It points toward a single piece of information. This can be to a place within the text or it can be a cross-reference to somewhere else within the index. A single entry can contain multiple levels of subheadings, so long as it only has one locator. An entry may also be called a record.

The following are all examples of a single entry:

Jasper National Park, 34
national parks
    Jasper National Park, 34
parks. *See* national parks

ARRAYS

An array, in contrast to an entry, contains everything that the index has to say about a particular subject. If there is only one place in the book where the subject is discussed, then a single entry will also constitute a single array. For example,

> fashion, 98

If the subject is discussed in multiple places, requiring multiple entries, then the entries combined under a single main heading constitute a single array. The following array contains one main heading, four subheadings, three cross-references, and fourteen entries (which I determined by counting the number of locators and cross-references).

> fashion
>   brands, 43, 56–58
>   labor practices, 2, 67, 70–74
>   models, 53, 85–88, 98
>   supply chains, 34–36, 45, 87
>   *See also* American Apparel; Chanel; Paris Fashion Week

Please note that I am making an editorial choice in how the terms entry and array are defined. Some indexers and indexing books use the terms interchangeably, or use the term entry to mean array. I have also seen used the term entry array.

Whatever your stance on terminology, I think that the distinction between the smaller unit and the larger unit is useful. It adds clarity for when I am discussing a specific entry compared to a larger array.

MAIN HEADINGS

The main heading is the term that explains what this thing is about. They should be clear and specific so that readers do not need to guess the meaning. Main headings may also be called main entries or simply headings.

Main headings are typically nouns—people, places, organizations, concepts. If the main heading needs to be modified in order to clarify the meaning of the entry, lead with the key term. For example, "eating habits of three-toed sloths," for which three-toed sloths are the focus of discussion, should be rewritten as "three-toed sloths, eating habits of."

SUBHEADINGS

Subheadings, also known as subentries, expand upon the main heading. They add an additional level of detail, allowing the user to narrow their search. The relationship between main heading and subheading should be easy to understand.

In an entry or array, the subheading follows the main heading. While an array can contain a single subheading, it is more common for an array to contain multiple subheadings, breaking down a discussion into smaller chunks.

While subheadings should be clear and specific, there is more flexibility in how to phrase them. Conjunctions and prepositions, such as *and*, *on*, *of*, *in*, and *against*, can help to indicate the relationship to the main heading, though are not always necessary. As seen below, subheadings can also be descriptive phrases, rather than a single term. The subheading should be concise while also being clear and providing enough information for the reader to understand the meaning.

There are a few reasons for using subheadings.

One is when there is a long discussion, spanning several pages, and it is helpful to the reader to know the components of that discussion. This occurred in *A Trillion Trees*, by Fred Pearce. A discussion about the biotic pump, which is a global network of winds driven by forests, spanned seven pages, which, depending on the book and audience, can be a long range to ask readers to search within. A common rule of thumb is to add subheadings if the range is more than five pages. I therefore added the following subheadings to this array:

> biotic pump
>   cold Amazon paradox and, 55
>   proof for, 55–57
>   resistance to, 54–55
>   Russia's Forest Code and, 57–58
>   theory development, 52–54

A related scenario is when the text contains clear subsections that can be replicated in the index. An example of this is from *Best Places to Bird in British Columbia*, a bird-watching guide by Russell Cannings and Richard Cannings. Each chapter profiled a different location and contained three distinct sections. I decided to replicate that structure in the index with the same subheadings for each place.

> Vaseux Lake
>   introduction, 109–10
>   birding guide, 110–14
>   getting there, 111

Subheadings can also be used to differentiate between similar yet distinct elements or concepts. In the index for *Best Places to Bird in British Columbia*, I also had the following array:

> Swallow
>   Northern Rough-winged, 33
>   Tree, 97–98
>   Violet-green, 97–98, 113

Since these are all swallows, the array could have been written as "swallows, 33, 97–98, 113," but that would have erased the distinctions between the different species. I decided that the primary audience for this book, birdwatchers, would appreciate a more granular approach, and so I used subheadings to differentiate.

A final scenario for using subheadings is for recurring mentions that generate a long string of page references. A long string of undifferentiated references can be a big ask for readers. Without more information, some readers may be discouraged from looking up each page, as they are not sure how long it will take to find relevant information. The solution is to pre-filter the page references using subheadings, so that readers can clearly see what the different discussions are about.

I did this for the "community and relationships" array for *Personal Next*, by Melinda Harrison. The concept is important, appearing throughout the book in different contexts and on fifteen different pages, or nine distinct locators. I decided that that was enough to justify subheadings, and so I used subheadings to highlight the different ways in which community and relationships appeared.

> community and relationships
>   changes when all-in, 52
>   competition within relationships, 126
>   creating connections, 143–44, 165
>   emotional support for reducing stress, 146
>   inner circle, 61–63
>   loss of protective bubble, 92–93
>   loss of social structures, 93–94
>   when testing the waters, 33–35

There is no hard or fast rule for how many references justify subheadings. Part of the calculation is determining the relative importance of the main heading. Another consideration, like in the swallows example, is what type of information is being differentiated. For scholarly books, I usually add subheadings if there are more than six or seven references, while for trade books, for a general audience, I may bump the bar up to seven or eight references. Other indexers have their own rules of thumb. The one constant is that subheadings should provide clarity. They should be clearly written and can make a large amount of information more accessible.

LOCATORS

Locators are the final element in the entry, coming after the main heading and subheading. The locator directs readers to where information is found. In this section, I will discuss the basic elements and considerations for locators. For a more in-depth discussion of undifferentiated and unruly locators, see page 123.

For books, locators are usually page numbers using Arabic numerals (1, 2, 3). However, some publishers use roman numerals (iv, v, vi) for the frontmatter, such as the table of contents (not indexable), the preface (sometimes indexable), and maybe the introduction (often indexable). If these pages contain material that readers may search for in the index, then these pages are indexable, and the locators in the index will include both roman and Arabic numerals. When sorting the locators, place the roman numerals first, and make sure that the roman numerals are in the correct order.

sunlight, iii, xiv–xv, 11-12, 132

While locators are usually page numbers, they do not have to be. The index for the *Chicago Manual of Style* is an excellent example of section numbers being used. Paragraph or line numbers may also be applicable. For journals or multivolume works, volume numbers can be added to the page numbers. For policy documents, policy numbers may be the best choice, while for audiovisual material, time stamps can be used. Once, for an internal document for an organization, I even used employee's names. Locators can be anything, so long as the meaning is clear to the index user.

Use commas to separate locators from one another, as well as from main headings and subheadings. Ranges, whether across pages or paragraphs or some other unit, are used to indicate a continuous discussion. Use an en dash to hold ranges together.

Publishers may also want ranges to be abbreviated, which saves space. The two most common approaches are *Chicago Manual of Style* and *New Hart's Rules*. Examples of each are below, compared to uncompressed ranges. Check with your publisher for their preference. The index should also match how page ranges are handled elsewhere in the book, such as in the bibliography.

> Unabbreviated ranges: 34–35, 99–101, 102–103, 145–146, 167–172
> *Chicago Manual of Style* abbreviation guidelines: 34–35, 99–101, 102–3, 145–46, 167–72
> *New Hart's Rules* abbreviation guidelines: 34–5, 99–101, 102–3, 145–6, 167–72

Locators can also be modified to indicate special elements within the text. Figures, tables, maps, and other illustrations can be highlighted by placing the locator in bold or italics, or by appending a note to the locator, such as a fig. or (t). Footnotes and endnotes can be indicated by adding an n along with the note number (for example, the note numbered three on page 52 would be indicated by 52n3). If two or more notes are in a row, then append a double nn and a range linking the note numbers. Here are a few examples of modified locators.

> Acura NSX, 45–47, 47(t)
> Dodge Charger, 23–25, 26*fig*.
> Ford Focus, 76, **94**
> Nissan Versa, *79–80*, 81, 97
> Subaru Forester, 45, 109, 159n34, 160nn44–46

Check with your publisher for instructions on how to indicate these elements. Because of the different ways that locators for figures, tables, maps, and other illustrations can be presented, it is also a good idea to include a headnote—a brief note at the beginning of the index—to explain your choice.

CROSS-REFERENCES

Cross-references direct readers to related information. It is a way to help readers navigate within the index.

There are two types of cross-references, *See* and *See also*. *See* references direct readers to the preferred term, where all the relevant locators can be found. For example, when there are two or more synonymous terms for the same concept or object. The text may use these terms interchangeably, or, if the text consistently uses a single term, you as the indexer may be aware that some readers may search under alternative terms.

Say that the preferred term in the book is Indigenous Peoples, but you are aware that Aboriginal Peoples, First Nations, and/or Native Americans are also terms, commonly or previously used, which readers are likely to search. In the index, Indigenous Peoples becomes the main array, and the other terms are included with a *See* reference. This way, readers will find the correct main entry regardless of how they search.

> Aboriginal Peoples. *See* Indigenous Peoples
> ...
> First Nations. *See* Indigenous Peoples
> ...
> Indigenous Peoples ...
> ...
> Native Americans. *See* Indigenous Peoples

Terms that are used interchangeably in the text can be handled two ways. One option is to choose a term to use as the primary array in the index, with *See* references redirecting from the other terms. The preferred term could be the term used most frequently in the text or the term that you think most of the audience will think of first. If terminology has changed over time, this could also be the most up-to-date and sensitive term.

Alternatively, if the terms have slightly different nuances, are associated with different scholars, or it otherwise seems important to keep separate, then treat each term as a separate array, with locators, and use *See also* references to indicate that additional discussions also exist under similar terms.

See also references can also be used to showcase other types of related terms within the index, in addition to synonyms. These relationships are usually either associative or hierarchical.

Associative relationships are terms within the same general area, and thinking about one term may cause the reader to think about and be interested in similar terms. For example, a reader looking up doctors may also be interested in main entries for other types of health care workers, and vice versa.

Hierarchical relationships are usually from broader terms to more specific terms. A book discussing taxation, for example, may have separate discussions for different types of taxes. Each type will have their own array, and cross-references from "taxes" can redirect readers to each type. This could be a *See* reference, if there are no other locators under "taxes," or, if there is some general information about taxes, a *See also* reference.

Associative and hierarchical cross-references can also be used together. Under "taxes," *See* references direct readers toward the specific types of taxes, while the *See also* references under each specific type point readers to related arrays.

> corporate tax, ... *See also* income tax; sales tax
> ...
> income tax, ... *See also* corporate tax; sales tax
> ...
> sales tax, ... *See also* corporate tax; income tax
> ...
> taxes. *See* corporate tax; income tax; sales tax

Cross-references can also redirect from a subheading. This is less commonly done, but useful if that level of precision seems necessary. Continuing with the tax example, say that only income tax has a sufficiently large discussion to require a separate array. The "taxes" array might, then, look like this:

> taxes
>   corporate tax, 45, 56–58, 99–102, 133
>   income tax (*see* income tax)
>   sales tax, 34, 46–48

Cross-references can also be general, as in "*See also specific types of taxes.*" This assumes that readers will know all the types of taxes being discussed. This can also be used to save space, if there would otherwise be a long list of cross-references. For the most part, though, it is better to be specific and not to assume that readers will understand what the general cross-reference refers to.

The goal for all cross-references is to anticipate how readers might search and what readers might want to know, and then clearly direct readers to the relevant arrays.

When editing the index, double-check that the cross-reference is accurate and correct. The suggested array should exist, and the cross-reference should use the same phrasing as the main heading it is pointing toward. Also ensure that the cross-reference points toward new information. If the recommended array simply repeats the same locators, then the cross-reference is unnecessary. For example, separate arrays for autumn and fall serve both types of readers. If both arrays contain the same set of locators, then redirecting from one to another does not add value.

When formatting, place *See* and *See also* in italics. This visually distinguishes them from the other elements in the array. The exception is if the cross-referenced term is itself in italics. For example, "*See also* L'Engle, Madeleine" versus "*See also A Wrinkle in Time* (L'Engle)." If cross-references are placed at the main heading level, then *See* and *See also* should be capitalized. If at the subheading level, then lowercase and placed in parentheses. At the main heading level, cross-references are usually placed at the end of the array, after the locators or after all the subheadings, though cross-references can also be placed immediately after the main heading. Placing after the main heading may be helpful if it is important for readers to immediately see all the other arrays in the index that may also be relevant, instead of first having to scan all the subheadings. A period precedes the cross-reference, and there is no closing punctuation.

TAKEAWAYS

- Indexes are composed of a few basic components: entries, arrays, main headings, subheadings, locators, and cross-references.

- Entries and arrays are helpful for conceptualizing the different units within an index and how these units fit together to create the larger whole.

- Main headings and subheadings explain to readers what this bit of information is about. These should be clearly written, with no ambiguity.

- Locators direct readers to information contained within the text or elsewhere in the index. Page numbers are the most common, though, depending on the material, other types of locators may be appropriate too.

- Cross-references direct readers to a different location in the index. They are important for making sure that readers get to the right place.

- In a well-written index, each element works together to clearly present and direct readers to the information in the book or document.

TRY THIS

Reach for the stack of books you previously selected. Try to find these six components in the indexes. Examine the indexes on their own and compare the indexes to each other. Hopefully, the books you have selected contain examples of both well-written and poorly written indexes, allowing you to get a feel for what works and what does not work.

- Can you identify entries and arrays? How easy or difficult is it to read the arrays? Comparing the indexes to each other, what factors might be involved?
- Are main headings clearly written? Do you understand what the entry or array is about?
- Are subheadings clearly written? Does the relationship between the main heading and subheading make sense? Do subheadings seem thoughtfully or randomly chosen?
- What is used for locators? Are any locators modified to indicate elements such as figures and tables? If yes, is the meaning of that modification clearly indicated and understandable? Are page ranges compressed?
- Are cross-references used? Are they for associative or hierarchical relationships, or both? Are the cross-references relevant?

3

Term Selection: What is Your Book About?

TERM SELECTION IS ONE OF the most important aspects of indexing. Without clearly written terms, at both the main heading and subheading levels, readers will have a difficult time finding the information they seek. Selecting terms is also about anticipating the needs of the index users.

In this chapter, I will discuss how to select terms, especially in relationship to the hierarchy of information that exists in every book. Once terms are selected, they then need to be organized into a structure, which I discuss in chapter 4.

AUDIENCE: WHO IS THE INDEX FOR?

An index is always written for someone. Sometimes, that someone is ourselves, such as an index for a favorite cookbook that lacks a good index or a document at work that is frequently referenced. More often, though, the index is written for someone else, and the needs of that audience should guide the terms that the index includes.

The flip side to not considering the audience's needs is that anything and everything is indexable. This can quickly lead to a sprawling index which may be too long for the space allotted, and may be too difficult to search because it is bloated with irrelevant terms.

When thinking about term selection, start with the audience. It may be that a highly detailed index does meet the user's needs; I am not trying to advocate for a specific length or style. I am saying that the index should be appropriate to its audience.

That said, it can be difficult to know who, exactly, that audience is. Books can have a wide variety of readers, with needs that may not occur to us. If you are not sure, one option is to ask the author or the publisher, as they will often have an intended audience in mind. From my own experience, I also often use the following guidelines for different types of books.

Scholarly books are often written for other academics and contain carefully constructed arguments and extensive documentation and evidence. The index should be similarly detailed, covering the arguments, documentation, and the scholars discussed. Disciplines can have their own jargon and terms of art that can be used as main entries with the assumption that readers in the field are familiar with those terms.

Trade books, in contrast, can vary considerably in their audience's needs. Some books, intended more for leisure or audiences less familiar with the subject, can have a lighter, less detailed index. Index entries are focused more on the big picture. While jargon used within the book can be replicated in the index, the index should also use terms that are accessible to readers who are less familiar with the subject matter. Other trade books may require detailed indexes, slanted in a certain direction. A gardening book, for example, should focus on plants and gardening techniques, while a how-to guide should ensure that all steps are easily found.

Some books and documents exist primarily as a resource and will not be read cover to cover. These include encyclopedias, cookbooks, guidebooks, handbooks, and policies. Because the index will often be the first point of entry for readers looking for a specific piece of information, these indexes should be detailed and comprehensive, with a lot of subheadings, so that readers can quickly pinpoint the information they want.

Books can also have multiple audiences. Some scholarly books may have crossover appeal in the trade market. Wildlife handbooks may be used by both professionals and amateur enthusiasts. For these books, the index should include entries and terms appropriate for all audiences.

I faced this situation when I indexed *Our Whole Gwich'in Way of Life Has Changed / Gwich'in K'yuu Gwiidandài' Tthak Ejuk Gòonlih*, by Leslie McCartney and the Gwich'in Tribal Council. The book is a collection of oral history interviews with twenty-three Gwich'in Elders from the Northwest Territories, Canada. The book is also published by a university press, and includes an extensive introduction, conclusion, appendix on the research process, and footnotes, all of which I indexed. One audience is scholarly, for those wanting to do research on the Gwich'in, as well as to understand the research process. Another important audience are the Gwich'in themselves. Many of the Elders told their stories specifically to pass on their family histories and traditional knowledge, with details including topics such as genealogies, their traditional land, hunting and food, and their lives in the present day. This is an invaluable resource for their descendants and others in the community. I decided that it was important to pick up all the names of people and places, even minor references, as well as details about everyday life that may seem insignificant but which the Elders included for a reason.

When indexing, the audience matters. Use the audience as a filter to help decide which terms to use, as well as how detailed or light the index should be.

ABOUTNESS AND THE HIERARCHY OF INFORMATION

Every book is about something. Every book also contains a structure, which, in the context of indexing, I like to call the hierarchy of information. Both what the book is about and the hierarchy of information need to be reflected in the index.

At the top of the hierarchy is the metatopic, which is what the book as a whole is about. Next are the supermain discussions, which are the handful or more main discussions that flesh out the metatopic. In turn, the supermain discussions can be broken down into the regular discussions. At the bottom of the hierarchy are all the little details. These are typically the names, concepts, and examples that illustrate or give authority to the supermain and regular discussions. Outside of the hierarchy, there may also be significant insignificant details (indexable) and passing mentions (not indexable). In the rest of the chapter, I will go into more detail explaining each of these elements.

The hierarchy of information is a rich source of terms. The index should contain main headings that correspond to each level. This accomplishes two goals: the index covers the full breadth of information contained in the text, and the book's readers will be able to find relevant information regardless of which level they search.

The alternative to indexing to the hierarchy of information is to treat the index as a simple list of names and concepts. This approach often assumes that terms are easily found via keyword search. But an index is more than just a list. A good index will show the relationship between terms, often through subheadings. A good index will also use a variety of terms—some more broad, others more specific—in order to reflect the range of the discussion and to provide multiple access points. For example, an index for a book on Islam in Western Europe should probably have arrays for Islam and Western Europe (the broadest level), as well as arrays for specific countries, ethnic groups, Islamic leaders, and Islamic organizations. Treating the index as a list risks glossing over the complexity of the text, whereas if you see the index as a reflection of the text, and understand that the text is composed of a specific structure, then you can mirror that structure and complexity in the index.

Circling back to aboutness, aboutness is simply recognizing what the book, at all levels of the hierarchy of information, is about. This is a useful concept because the aboutness of a section or paragraph is not always explicitly stated, yet still needs to be accurately reflected. Ask yourself: "If I need to explain to someone what this book/chapter/section/paragraph/sentence is about, what would I say?" When you have your answer, put it in the index.

Identifying the Hierarchy of Information

The hierarchy of information is not always obvious. It is one thing to understand that it exists; it can be another to identify it.

I find that I read differently when I index. I am actively reading, which is different from reading for pleasure and different from how I read in university. In university, I sought information and arguments for use in my papers and on exams, but I was not paying attention to how the text itself was constructed. When indexing, I am searching for key terms. If a key term is not obvious, I am reading between the lines and asking what this section is about. I am also looking for relationships, trying to understand how paragraphs, sections, and chapters all relate to each other. Reading like this is a skill that I gradually developed.

As you learn to index, also pay attention to how you read. Being able to identify the hierarchy of information is crucial for selecting terms and for seeing how the index might be structured.

After you read this chapter, spend some time practicing. Examine a few books and try to identify the metatopic, supermain discussions, and a few of the regular discussions and little bits. Draw a mind map or diagram to illustrate the interrelationships between the discussions.

An index is often compared to a map. In order to write an accurate map, you first need to know the terrain, or in this case, the text.

METATOPIC

Applied to indexing by Do Mi Stauber, the metatopic is simply what the book as a whole is about. It is the big picture, the topic under which all other discussions fall. It differs from aboutness in that determining aboutness is applicable to all levels of the hierarchy of information, whereas the metatopic is focused on the broadest level.

Some books have a simple metatopic. For *The Hidden Life of Trees*, by Peter Wohlleben, the metatopic is clearly stated in the title: trees.

For the biography *Railroader: The Unfiltered Genius and Controversy of Four-Time CEO Hunter Harrison,* by Howard Green, the metatopic is Hunter Harrison.

Other books have a more complicated metatopic. The book *Margaret Laurence and Jack McClelland, Letters,* edited by Laura K. Davis and Linda M. Morra, is about the relationship, as expressed through their letters, between these two individuals. This is a dual metatopic, or a metatopic with two equal aspects, around which the index will revolve. An example of a more complicated metatopic is *Mountains of Blame: Climate and Culpability in the Philippine Uplands,* by Will Smith. This metatopic requires a sentence to describe, which is blame and culpability for climate change in the context of the Indigenous Pala'wan people and Palawan Island, Philippines. All these elements are woven together and need to be reflected in the index. It is inaccurate to say that the book is simply about climate change or simply about the Pala'wan people or simply about the Philippines.

Being the first level in the hierarchy of information, the metatopic should be represented in the index by a metatopic array or arrays. Indexing practice on this has changed over the years. Since every entry in the book is potentially a subentry under the metatopic, the conventional wisdom used to be to exclude the metatopic and to only index the smaller units of discussion. Now, there is acknowledgment that many readers will search for the metatopic, and so a metatopic array is necessary, if only as a signpost to redirect readers elsewhere. Readers should not be left wondering why an index for a book on trees has nothing to say about trees.

When the metatopic is not clear and you are feeling stuck or lost, try stepping away from the text and summarizing the book in a sentence or two. Identify the different elements of the discussion and how they relate to each other. Think broadly, looking for elements that apply to the whole book, and not just to specific chapters. I often find this exercise helpful for clarifying what the book is about. Once I have that summary, I can extract terms for the index. For *Mountains of Blame,* for example, I created the following main headings to reflect the metatopic: "blame, for climate change," "climate change," "Palawan Island," "Pala'wan people," and "Philippines."

SUPERMAIN DISCUSSIONS AND HEADINGS

Supermain discussions, a term I learned from Margie Towery, are the key discussions of the book. Supermains flesh out the metatopic, and are the second level in the hierarchy of information. Often, a book is structured so that each chapter discusses a separate supermain discussion, though sometimes supermain discussions require two or more chapters or appear as recurring themes throughout the book.

The book *Uplift: Visual Culture at the Banff School of Fine Arts*, by PearlAnn Reichwein and Karen Wall, is a history and critical analysis of the Banff School of Fine Arts. Its supermain discussions, which each receive a chapter, are artist-teachers, students, extension (adult) education, branding, campus development, landscape and landscape painting, Indigenous Peoples, and tourism. These discussions bring the metatopic to life, and each becomes a main heading in the index.

There is no set number for how many supermain discussions a book may have. There are often just a handful, maybe upwards to a dozen. The key is that these are all high-level discussions, directly relating to the metatopic, and that supermain discussions are usually composed of their own set of smaller discussions.

REGULAR DISCUSSIONS AND HEADINGS

In the same way that supermain discussions expand on and illustrate the metatopic, regular discussions expand on and flesh out supermain discussions. These constitute the third level in the hierarchy of information.

Regular discussions are usually much shorter, though still important to index. If a supermain discussion can fill an entire chapter, then regular discussions may be the sections that subdivide the chapter, composed of upwards to a handful of pages each. Be careful, though—not every book is so clearly structured. While the book's structure, and its chapters and headings, can provide guidance for what the supermain and regular discussions are, it is important to actually read and track what the text is about.

Let's look again at *Uplift* and the Banff School of Fine Arts. The chapter on artist-teachers, which is a supermain discussion, contained discussions on compensation, gender, instructional approaches, networks among artists, and teachers as tourist attractions. These are all shorter discussions that expand the reader's understanding of artist-teachers. In the index, these can become subheadings within the artist-teachers array, as well as standalone main headings. This is called double-posting and allows these discussions to be found regardless of how the reader chooses to search, either more broadly or narrowly.

> artist-teachers
>   networks among, 179–181
> ...
> networks, art, 179–181

Note that some of the regular discussions can appear in multiple contexts. In *Uplift*, gender is also discussed in relation to students, and tourism is a supermain discussion in its own right. Combine these references from throughout the book into the appropriate arrays, so that each array provides an accurate overview for how and where the topic is discussed. One of the strengths of the index is that it can highlight these connections, which may be more difficult to see within the text.

ALL THE LITTLE BITS

At the bottom of the hierarchy of information are all the specific details which bolster and give life to the discussions: people, places, organizations, programs, concepts, and items. They may appear throughout the text in different contexts, and will likely just be discussed in

> ### Are People and Things Always at the Bottom of the Hierarchy?
>
> I wish it were that simple, that different types of information can be reliably matched to different levels of the hierarchy of information. But every book is different.
>
> The hierarchy of information is simply a framework for understanding how books are structured. While in some books there may be a clear divide between upper-level concepts being discussed and lower-level people and things being used to illustrate and support, the reality is that people, places, organizations, programs, concepts, and items can appear at every level. In a corporate history, for example, the metatopic is the organization being discussed. Key leaders in the organization may be supermain or regular discussions.
>
> As you index, pay attention to what the book is about. As you figure that out, you will be able to map out the hierarchy, which will help inform the terms used in the index and the index structure.

a few sentences or paragraphs. These are also important to index for those readers looking for a specific example or an important person in the field.

These smaller details are often easy to identify and to pick up. They are usually concrete and clearly labeled, used to illustrate or prove a point. A common pitfall is to think that the index is solely composed of these smaller entries. It is important to understand the hierarchy of information and to index at all levels, so that the full breadth of the book is indexed.

SIGNIFICANT INSIGNIFICANT DETAILS

Significant insignificant details, a term I learned from Mary Newberry, are details that are not directly related to the main discussion yet may still be of interest. This is about seeing the text from a different perspective and considering what else might be relevant. For example, indexing wildlife in a book on Arctic exploration, or details about uniforms in a book on the Battle of Gettysburg. Wildlife or uniforms are not what the book is about, and probably do not even directly support the supermain or regular discussions. But there is still sufficient information for a reader to learn something meaningful.

Significant insignificant details tie into the fact that most indexes have multiple audiences. Different audiences will be interested in different things. Stepping outside the hierarchy of information, consider what else the text is about. Are there additional interesting nuggets of information which are worth highlighting?

PASSING MENTIONS

In contrast to all the little bits and significant insignificant details, passing mentions should not be indexed. Passing mentions are items that are not discussed in and of themselves, nor does the reader learn anything substantial about them. Instead, passing mentions usually appear in support of other information.

Utilize aboutness to help identify what is indexable and to separate out passing mentions. Focus on the purpose of the passage, and then consider whether what is left is indexable. In some cases, what is left will be significant insignificant details and in other cases passing mentions.

I admit that identifying passing mentions is somewhat subjective, and is a skill that may take some practice. What counts as a passing mention will also vary from book to book, depending on the scope and audience of the index. It's okay if it takes practice for this to make sense. Just remember the two key questions: is something substantial learned about this person or thing, and is this relevant to a potential reader?

Let's see how this decision making plays out in an example from *Uplift*:

TERM SELECTION: WHAT IS YOUR BOOK ABOUT?

Through the Banff School, instructors participated in a network of colleagues, institutions, organizations, and classrooms across the province and beyond, and they exhibited widely in venues that ranged from community halls to galleries. J. B. Taylor, a protégé of [Henry George] Glyde from Ontario, taught at the school in spring, summer, and fall sessions from 1948 until 1954. He also co-founded the Alberta Society of Education through the Arts, served on the Provincial Arts Board, and exemplified the devotion of many to extension education as he travelled to towns all over Alberta in the winter, sometimes taking one of his sons with him.

This passage is part of the regular discussion about art networks, and is also about J. B. Taylor. Entries can be made for both, to direct readers to what this passage is about. Since this passage is also about artist-teachers (or instructors), networks can also be a subheading under the artist-teachers array.

There are other pieces of information in this passage for which aboutness is less clear. Is Henry George Glyde indexable? The only piece of information we learn is that Taylor was his protégé. I decided that that was relevant information about Glyde, especially as Glyde is also discussed elsewhere in the book. In contrast, I did not create entries for the Alberta Society of Education through the Arts or the Provincial Arts Board. These are the only mentions in the book, I did not think that enough substantial information was provided, nor do these institutions tie into the metatopic, which is the Banff School of Fine Arts. A good rule of thumb is, will a reader be satisfied with the information they are pointed toward? In this case, I decided no. That said, this was a judgment call that I made, and it is okay if you would have decided differently.

Other passing mentions in this passage are, in my opinion, clearly not indexable. Ontario, for example, is simply mentioned to provide context for Glyde. The reader otherwise learns nothing about that province. Similarly, Taylor's unnamed son is not indexable, since this is the only reference and is only mentioned to give a better sense of Taylor's travels.

BUILDING A HOUSE

Indexers like to use a variety of metaphors to describe writing an index. Creating a map to the text is a common one, as is piecing together a puzzle. Right now, consider constructing the index as building a house.

The metatopic forms the foundations upon which the whole house sits. The supermain arrays are the beams and framing that provide structure and support, but are, by themselves, not enough to keep out the wind and rain. The regular arrays are the walls and roof, giving the house it's solidity. All the little bits are the details like paint, doors, windows, and other fittings which transform the house from a shell into a functional home. The significant insignificant details are perhaps the knickknacks and decorations that are not strictly necessary, but which help give the home its distinctiveness.

All the information in a book is interrelated and exists to support each other. These relationships need to be mirrored in the index. Part of this is extracting relevant terms for each level in the hierarchy of information, which become the main headings and subheadings in the index. The other part is using the hierarchy of information to inform the structure of the index, which I discuss in the next chapter.

TAKEAWAYS

- Term selection is the process of determining what will be the main headings and subheadings in the index.

- Indexes are always written for someone, and that audience, or multiple audiences, should influence which terms are selected.

- Aboutness is understanding what the text, at all levels, is about. The terms used in the index should accurately reflect the text.

- The hierarchy of information is a framework for understanding how books are organized. In addition to aboutness, terms should also correspond to each level of the hierarchy of information.

- The metatopic is what the whole book is about. It can be simple, described in a word or two, or contain multiple elements, requiring a sentence or two to explain.
- Supermain discussions are the main discussions of the book, fleshing out the metatopic.
- Regular discussions are smaller discussions which flesh out the supermain discussions.
- All the little details are the lowest level of discussions, in support of supermain and regular discussions.
- Significant insignificant details are not directly relevant to the metatopic, but still contain enough information to potentially be of interest to a reader.
- Passing mentions are details that are not relevant. Not enough substantive information is present to warrant including in the index.

TRY THIS

Reach again for those books you are perusing for practice.

- Who is the audience? Does the index seem appropriate for that audience?
- Can you identify the metatopic? Try summarizing the book in a couple of words or a sentence or two. Can you find a metatopic array or arrays in the index?
- Try outlining or creating a diagram of the hierarchy of information. What are some of the supermain discussions? Regular discussions? Some of the little bits? This diagram or list does not need to be exhaustive. Just practice identifying the different elements.
- Can you find arrays in the index that correspond to these different levels? How well does the index reflect the relationships within the book?

Think about the book that you are indexing.

- Again, who is the audience? What might your audience want, in terms of how detailed or comprehensive the index should be, and/or in terms of specific types of information?
- What is the metatopic? Write it down. What main heading or headings can you derive from this?
- What are the supermain discussions? How can these be rephrased as main headings?
- What are some of the regular discussions? All the little bits? Significant insignificant details? Jot down a few examples of each. Practice seeing the text in these terms so that you will be more prepared for when you start indexing.
- Try creating a mind map to express the interrelationships. A mind map is a diagram for showing relationships between terms. Start with the metatopic in the center and work outwards. This can help you see a big-picture view of the book's contents and how everything fits together. It may also help you differentiate between supermain and regular discussions, and how regular discussions may connect to multiple supermains.

4

Structure: Putting the Pieces Together

IDENTIFYING AND UNDERSTANDING INDEX STRUCTURE is tough. Many professional indexers struggle with structure early in their career, and it may take writing several indexes before it starts to make sense.

And that's okay.

Structure is, essentially, how all the entries and arrays fit together. It is making a home for each piece of information, while also directing readers to the right place. A good structure should make information accessible.

In this chapter, I will discuss how structure can also be mapped to the hierarchy of information. This is seen most clearly in the table of contents approach, but also when the book's structure is less clear. I also discuss providing multiple access points.

As you read this chapter, think about which approach might be most appropriate for your book.

BUILDING FROM THE TABLE OF CONTENTS

Some books have a very clear structure, which may be outlined in an extensive table of contents and also clearly spelled out in chapter and section titles that speak directly to that section's aboutness. In my experience, how-to guides are often like this, as are scholarly books in the social sciences. These books can be easier to index because the structure is in plain sight.

These books have an easy-to-identify metatopic. The supermain discussions are also clearly labeled, usually one per chapter. Each chapter, in turn, can be subdivided into clearly labeled regular discussions.

Consider *Wag: The Science of Making Your Dog Happy*, by Zazie Todd. The metatopic is how to take care of your pet dog. This becomes an array for "dogs."

Each chapter in this book focuses on a separate aspect of dog care. These are the supermain discussions, from which I derived the following subheadings for the metatopic array:

> dogs
>   introduction and conclusion, 1–7, 242–48
>   aging and special needs, 214–25
>   attachment to their humans, 111–24
>   with children, 125–37
>   choosing a dog, 20–41
>   dog training, 65–80
>   end-of-life issues, 226–41
>   enrichment, 152–65
>   food, 166–80
>   happiness, 8–19
>   learning by, 42–64
>   play and socialization, 97–110
>   problem behaviors, 196–213
>   sleep, 181–95
>   veterinarian visits, 81–96
>   walks, 138–51
>   *See also specific topics*

Note that the locator ranges are long, covering the entire chapter. Normally, such long ranges should be avoided, as smaller chunks of information are usually more useful for readers, but the metatopic array, in this structure, is a special case. Its purpose is to serve as a starting point and introduction for those readers who choose to search at the broadest level. This array provides, at a glance, all the main topics. Also notice the generic cross-reference at the bottom, "*See also specific topics,*" which indicate that these topics all have their own arrays, should the reader want to see the topic broken down into specific detail.

Moving down the hierarchy of information, each supermain discussion is double-posted as its own array. The chapter range is also duplicated, for those readers who want to read the whole chapter. The chapter range is then broken down into subheadings, for each of the regular discussions. For example, here is the array for sleep:

> sleep, 181–95
>   introduction, 181–82
>   alertness during, 188–90
>   amount needed, 186–88
>   applying the science at home, 195
>   co-sleeping, 182–84
>   dog beds, 184, 195
>   dreams during, 194–95
>   learning and, 191–93, 195
>   sleep patterns, 185–86
>   stressful events and, 190–91
>   twitching and whimpering during, 193–95

In the same way that supermain discussions are both standalone arrays and subheadings under the metatopic, regular discussions can also be double-posted. But here, there are a few more options.

Some subheadings can simply be double-posted as standalone arrays without further subheadings, as the discussion about these topics is limited. Here are examples from the sleep array:

> alertness, 188–90
> co-sleeping, 182–84
> dog beds, 184, 195
> dreams, 194–95

In contrast, learning is also a supermain discussion, and stress is discussed in other contexts, so sleep is double-posted as a subheading under those arrays:

```
learning
    sleep and, 191–93, 195
stress
    sleep and, 190–91
```

I did not double-post "introduction" or "applying the science at home," since these are summary sections in each chapter and only make sense in relation to their respective supermain discussions. I also did not double-post "amount needed" and "twitching and whimpering during" as these are so closely tied to sleep that I did not think readers would look these up independently, while "sleep patterns" would have sorted, alphabetically, immediately below "sleep," which is redundant.

Combined, the metatopic, supermain, and regular arrays and entries begin to look like an index. Though organized alphabetically, the arrays reflect the book's structure, and the entries cascade from the metatopic array to the supermain arrays to the regular arrays. Through double-posting, multiple access points are provided at the different levels, to accommodate how different readers may choose to search.

```
aging ...
alertness, 188–90
children ...
co-sleeping, 182–84
dog beds, 184, 185
dogs
    introduction and conclusion, 1–7, 242–48
    aging and special needs, 214–25
    attachment to their humans, 111–24
    with children, 125–37
    choosing a dog, 20–41
    dog training, 65–80
```

end-of-life issues, 226–41
enrichment, 152–65
food, 166–80
happiness, 8–19
learning by, 42–64
play and socialization, 97–110
problem behaviors, 196–213
sleep, 181–95
veterinarian visits, 81–96
walks, 138–51
See also specific topics
dogs, choosing ...
dog training ...
dreams, 194–195
end-of-life issues ...
enrichment ...
food ...
happiness ...
humans, attachment to ...
learning ...
   sleep and, 191–93, 195
play ...
problem behaviors ...
sleep, 181–95
   introduction, 181–82
   alertness during, 188–90
   amount needed, 186–88
   applying the science at home, 195
   co-sleeping, 182–84
   dog beds, 184, 195
   dreams during, 194–95
   learning and, 191–93, 195
   sleep patterns, 185–86
   stressful events and, 190–91
   twitching and whimpering during, 193–95
socialization ...
stress ...
   sleep and, 190–91

veterinarian visits …
walks …

So far, this section has been about building a structure using the upper and midlevels of the hierarchy of information—the metatopic, supermain discussions, and regular discussions. These are the large building blocks, and a good structure will ensure that these elements are present and easy to find. But books are also composed of small details. These need to be picked up and incorporated too.

Let's revisit the metatopic array from *Wag*. While most of the subheadings are for chapter-length supermain discussions, I discovered a few smaller pieces of information that I thought were also relevant, and so I added a few more subheadings. Some of these, such as "canine science," "developmental stages," and "relinquishment," I also double-posted elsewhere in the index. So you can more easily see these additional subheadings, I have highlighted them in bold.

dogs
    introduction and conclusion, 1–7, 242–48
    aging and special needs, 214–25
    assistance for owners, 221–22
    attachment to their humans, 111–24
    author's experience with, 1–3, 6
    canine science, 5–6
    checklist for, 247–48, 249–52
    with children, 125–37
    choosing a dog, 20–41
    developmental stages, 32–33
    dog training, 65–80
    end-of-life issues, 226–41
    enrichment, 152–65
    estimated number of, 9
    food, 166–80
    happiness, 8–19
    learning about, 4–6, 175, 246–47
    learning by, 42–64

play and socialization, 97–110
problem behaviors, 196–213
reliance on humans, 58
relinquishment of, 239
sleep, 181–95
understanding point of view of, 123
veterinarian visits, 81–96
walks, 138–51
See also specific topics

Indexer Fred Leise calls this approach—both top-down and bottom-up—pan-granularity. Both are necessary. The starting point of structure is the top-down—making sure that all the major discussions have their place. Once that framework is created, then all the smaller details can be slotted in. If you are interested in learning more about Leise's approach, see the Resources on page 200.

A word of caution, however: not every book is so clearly organized. Ideally, you can quickly move through the text, creating the top-down structure of the metatopic, supermain discussions, and regular discussions, and then reread the book more slowly to pick up the details. But if chapter titles and section headings are not useful clues, or if the book is not organized in a systematic way that is easy to follow, it is easy to get bogged down and frustrated.

Before you begin indexing, first assess how the book is written and structured. If it seems to lend itself to a table-of-contents approach, great! If the book's structure is less clear, mapping the structure to the hierarchy of information is still applicable, but it will take a bit more work and may not look so tidy. I will discuss this more in the next section.

WHEN THE STRUCTURE IS LESS CLEAR

There are many reasons why a book's structure may be less clear. It could be that the underlying structure exists but is poorly labeled, often through chapter and section titles using jargon, descriptive, or otherwise

> ## Telling Readers Where to Start
>
> In the *Wag* example above, you may have noticed something odd about a couple of the arrays. The first subheading in the metatopic array is "introduction and conclusion," while the array for sleep begins with the subheading "introduction." Both of these subentries are sorted outside the normal alphabetical order. Why is that?
>
> Introductory material often appears at the beginning of a discussion, whether for the whole book, or a chapter, or a shorter section within a chapter. There may also be a conclusion. If subheadings are required, I usually place this introductory material at the beginning of the array as a way of saying to the reader, "Start here if you are not sure what you are looking for."
>
> I use a variety of subheadings to label these remarks: "about," "approach to," "introduction," "introduction and conclusion," "overview," or sometimes "summary." If the text consistently uses a particularly label for these sections, I will follow the book's lead. "About" will naturally sort to the top, which usually makes force-sorting unnecessary, but if the discussion feels more like an overview or a description of the author's approach, I will use those terms instead.
>
> Force-sorting is when main headings or subheadings are deliberately placed outside of the alphabetical sort. It should be done sparingly, so that readers can trust that entries will be where they expect, but placing a subheading for introductory material at the top of the array, however that subheading is phrased, is an exception I often make.

unclear language. It may also be that the supermain and regular discussions are not neatly divided into chapters and sections, and instead spill across chapters, requiring a closer reading. Themes may also be interwoven throughout the book. Another reason may be that the metatopic contains multiple elements, which makes it harder to map the metatopic to the index's structure. Different disciplines and genres can also have their own conventions governing book structure. These conventions are not wrong, as there are many ways to tell a story or present an argument, but some approaches can be easier to index than others.

Sometimes, an unclear book structure means that the book is poorly edited. If that is the case, and the book is ready for indexing, it is probably too late to revise the book (though you can ask!). Indexing is the art of working with whatever is on the page, well-written or not. As the indexer, you will need to read carefully and find a way to create order out of the chaos.

Despite a challenging book structure, the goal for the index structure remains to create an easy-to-follow map to the book's contents. A poor index structure can hinder the reader's use of it. Whether the challenge is a poorly or oddly structured book, a complicated metatopic, or multiple, interweaving elements, the hierarchy of information can still form the basic starting point.

In this section, I discuss four common scenarios: when there is extensive background discussion of the metatopic, when there is almost no discussion of the metatopic, when the metatopic is complicated, and when the book contains multiple, interweaving elements.

Metatopic Itself Extensively Discussed

Some metatopics require a lengthy introduction, before the book eventually gets to the supermain and regular discussions. In a way, this introductory material is itself a supermain discussion, since a lengthy array with subheadings will be required to parse the information.

This happened in *Masters and Servants: The Hudson's Bay Company and Its North American Workforce, 1668–1786*, by Scott P. Stephen. The metatopic is the North American workforce of the Hudson's Bay Company. The book begins with a long introduction, followed by chapters for each supermain discussion (in one case, two chapters to adequately cover a supermain discussion). Because there was so much background information about the Hudson's Bay Company, I decided to make that the metatopic array—the starting point. However, instead of creating subheadings with chapter-length locator ranges for each of the supermain discussions, as I did for *Wag*, I used the subheadings to provide an overview of the company and instead used cross-references to point readers to the supermain discussions.

> Hudson's Bay Company (HBC)
> approach to, xviii, xxx–xxxi, xxxvi, 273, 279–80
> Atlantic history and, xx–xxi, 291n22
> economic value for England, xvi
> employment, nature of, xxi–xxiii
> establishment, xii, 34
> foundational years, xiv, 32–36, 37–38, 40–42, 68
> French, conflict with, 42–50
> generational differences, 275–76
> graffiti left by employees, 120–21
> interloper concerns, 61, 311n102
> international commerce and influences, xv–xvi
> maritime service, xviii, 125, 323n42, 335n100
> military capabilities, xxvi–xxvii, 6, 34, 45–46, 48, 92–93, 161–62, 353n121
> physical isolation, xxix
> post-Utrecht expansion, 50–51, 68–69, 157, 313n125, 361n3
> purchases from company store, 113
> records, 9, 313n125, 329n15
> scholarly approaches to, xvii–xviii
> structure of, xii, xiv
> success attributed to employees, xvi
> terminology and occupational labels, 282, 285–87
> territorial holdings, legal basis for, 294n49
> trading posts, extent of, 362n6
> *See also* evaluation and retention; France and French traders; households; Indigenous Peoples; inland service; labor relations; marriage and sexual relations; master-servant relationship; private trade; recruitment; *specific forts*

Some of these subheadings establish a timeline, such as the subheadings for "establishment," "foundational years," and "post-Utrecht expansion." Others are double-posted elsewhere in the index, such as "Atlantic history" and "military capabilities." Some have to do with research, such as "records" and "scholarly approaches to." While a few, such as "graffiti left by employees" and "purchases from company store," didn't seem to fit anywhere else. There is a lot happening in this array. My concern was that too many subheadings would make the array difficult to read, so I decided to keep the focus relatively narrow, and place all the supermain discussions elsewhere.

While the metatopic array is handled differently, the arrays for supermain and regular discussions are much the same as for the table of contents approach. The larger discussion is broken down into subheadings, which are, in turn, double-posted as standalone arrays. I had to be careful, though, to track discussions. Even though supermain discussions were largely confined to specific chapters, discussions did sometimes spill over and appear elsewhere.

In this array for inland service, for example, some of the locators for the subheadings "concerns about," "early incursions," "expansion inland," and "French competition" are from much earlier in the book than most of the other locators. Notice that I am also continuing the broad-to-specific pattern, with the array being about inland service more generally, with cross-references pointing toward specific trading posts that are also relevant.

inland service
    introduction and conclusion, xxxi, 167–69, 191–92, 275–76
    concerns about, 64–65, 181, 183, 312n109
    contracts and wages, 190–91
    dissatisfaction among men, 189–90
    early incursions, 38, 40, 49–50, 61–62, 182–83, 312n103, 342n37
    expansion inland, 65–66, 69, 186–88
    French competition, 70, 181–82, 342n40
    Indigenous Peoples, staying with, 183–84, 185, 342n39
    private trade concerns, 183–85
    transportation and recruitment issues, 129–30
    See also Cumberland House; Henley House

Metatopics That Are Not Discussed

The opposite scenario is when the metatopic is rarely discussed and the focus is on the supermain discussions. This can happen in textbooks and edited collections, with the chapters loosely tied together around a single theme but otherwise independent. An example of this is the textbook *political science is for everybody: an introduction to political science*, edited by amy l. atchison. The chapters are wide-ranging, from comparative politics to international law to social movements, but I found the metatopic difficult to pin down. I eventually realized that it was politics (as opposed to the academic discipline of political science), yet very little, besides a definition, was directly said about politics. I decided that a metatopic array was still important as a starting point, but instead of listing each chapter as a subheading, I decided to follow the book's lead, with its emphasis on the supermain discussions, and simply redirect readers using cross-references. The metatopic array looked like this:

> politics, 14–15, 31. *See also* civil society; comparative politics; courts; democracy; electoral systems; executives; good life; human rights; ideology; international law; international organizations (IOs); international political economy (IPE); international relations (IR); intersectionality; legislatures; political behavior; political parties; political theory; public policy; representation; security; social movements

Complicated Metatopics

So far, the examples I have used have had simple metatopics that can be summed in a single main heading: dogs, Hudson's Bay Company, politics. But what about when the metatopic is too complicated to reduce to a single term? What if there are two or more elements and it is not clear where readers will start their search? The solution is to use multiple arrays to reflect the metatopic.

This was the case for *In the Present Moment: Buddhism, Contemporary Art, and Social Practice*, by Haema Sivanesan. The book is about Buddhism and artistic practice, which sounds simple, but is one element more important than the other? Both are valid entry points into the index, so I created the following arrays:

art
    action art, 147
    Buddha-nature and "everybody is an artist," 3, 131, 139–40
    Buddhism and contemporary art, 1–3, 71, 77, 125
    conceptual art, 7, 42, 47, 64, 77, 115
    Dalai Lama on, 126, 129
    dematerialization of, 31, 77, 78n21
    field principle, 115, 119
    importance of, 140
    individualism and, 23, 147
    life and, 64, 71
    process art, 40
    society as, 64, 67
    Thubten Yeshe on, 137–38
    See also Buddhism, and contemporary art; Fluxus; mandala; socially engaged art practice; *specific artists*
Buddhism, and contemporary art
    about, 1–3, 71, 77, 125
    acquiring an appropriate state of mind, 10, 14
    awareness practice, 28–29, 31
    Buddhism as artistic methodology, 2, 7, 23, 25, 77
    cross-cultural exchanges, 14, 18, 21
    cultural Buddhism, 45
    Dalai Lama on art, 126, 129
    "everybody is an artist" and Buddha-nature, 3, 131, 139–40
    modern Buddhism and, 2, 25, 27–28
    scholarship on, 4
    social practice and, 67–69, 71, 73–74
    Thubten Yeshe on art, 137–38
    See also Fluxus; mandala; socially engaged art practice; *specific artists*

These two arrays are distinct. They have different subheadings, with the "art" array more narrowly focused on art while the "Buddhism, and contemporary art" array is more focused on Buddhism's role. Yet there are also a few subheadings that overlap (bolded), to show that these two different subjects are related, and so that regardless of where readers begin, they will understand that this book is about both Buddhism and art. Both arrays also redirect readers to the same supermain discussions.

Some metatopics are even more complicated than this. In the metatopic discussion, in chapter three, I discussed the metatopic for *Mountains of Blame: Climate and Culpability in the Philippine Uplands*, by Will Smith, which is blame and culpability for climate change in the context of Palawan Island, Philippines, and the Indigenous Pala'wan people. I ended up creating arrays for each of the main elements: blame, for climate change; climate change; Palawan Island; Pala'wan people; and Philippines. Similar to *In the Present Moment*, each array was distinct while also sharing subheadings so that readers could see the interconnections and get a fuller picture of the book, regardless of where they started their search.

Multiple, Interweaving Elements

A final scenario is when the book contains multiple, interweaving elements. This is similar to a complicated metatopic, and it may be that a book has both a complicated metatopic and interweaving elements. In this scenario, though, I am focusing more on complicated supermain and regular discussions.

Most books can be described as multifaceted, in that there are a handful or more supermain discussions and several regular discussions. What I am describing is that, but supercharged. Instead of the supermain and regular discussions being relatively independent from each other, everything and everyone seems to be mixed up in each other's business.

Let's look at *Decolonizing Independence: Statecraft in Nigeria's First Republic and Israeli Interventions*, by Lynn Schler. The metatopic is straightforward. The book is about Israeli interventions in Nigeria during the First Republic period (approximately 1960–1966). What is complicated are all the different actors. Nigeria is divided into three main regions (North, East, and West). Each region has its own dominant political party, which contain one or more leaders who are extensively discussed. There is also tension between the federal government and the regional governments, and between the political parties and leaders. Israel, of course, is also involved with all these actors, and in specific projects that are discussed, such as joint corporations and the Farm Settlement Scheme. All these overlapping elements need arrays, and all these relationships need to be reflected in the index. Otherwise, the standalone arrays run the risk of creating silos, glossing over the interconnectedness that is an important part of the narrative.

The solution is to double-post (and even triple-, quadruple-, and quintuple-post) subheadings, so that readers can see the connections and get a glimpse of the full picture, regardless of where they start.

There are too many arrays to reproduce them all, so I will focus on a subset for the Action Group political party; its leader, Obafemi Awolowo; and the Western Region, the home base for both Action Group and Awolowo. Each array is unique, in that it focuses on its subject and contain subheadings that are not found elsewhere. Each array also shares subheadings with each other, as well as with other arrays in the index (bolded). These have to do with elections, Israeli relations, a leadership crisis, and specific projects such as joint corporations, shipping line negotiations, and Universal Primary Education. These are the interconnections between actors, and readers can access them from any one of these arrays.

Note, however, that the locators do not always match exactly. Each subheading is still tailored to its specific subject. While the Action Group and Awolowo were both involved with Israel, for example, often overlapping, there were times in which they acted independently from each other, which the index also reflects. Also note that how the subheadings are phrased is also tailored to the array, and are not always identical. For example, "leadership crisis and tensions between Akintola and Awolowo" under Action Group, and "Action Group leadership crisis and conflict with Akintola" under Awolowo. It is a good idea to keep wording similar, so readers can identify that these subheadings are about the same thing, while also allowing each array to be internally coherent.

> Action Group (AG)
>   introduction, xxxiii, 3
>   **1954 elections, 8**
>   **1959 elections, 27–28, 29–32, 58**
>   1960 loan agreement and, 43
>   background, 7
>   corruption allegations, 90–91
>   demise after Western Region Crisis, 135
>   development and modernist philosophy, 57, 61, 62, 63, 64
>   finances, 167n61
>   **Israeli relations, 3, 10–11, 12–14, 27–28, 53, 117, 147**
>   **Israeli special assistance for 1959 elections, 20–24, 27–28, 37–38, 147, 148**
>   **joint corporations and, 24–25, 26–27, 52, 55–56, 90–91**
>   Lagos and, 9
>   **leadership crisis and tensions between Akintola and Awolowo, 83, 86–90, 91**
>   minority rights and, 9, 20
>   Okotie-Eboh against, 40
>   **shipping line negotiations and, 19–20**
>   **Universal Primary Education program, 61, 69–70**
>   Yavor and, xxx
>   Yoruba and, 6–7, 58
>   See also Awolowo, Obafemi; Coker Commission of Inquiry; Farm Settlement Scheme; joint corporations; Western Region
> Awolowo, Obafemi
>   **1954 elections and, 8**
>   **1959 election campaign, 29–32**
>   **Action Group leadership crisis and conflict with Akintola, 83, 86–91**
>   backstage negotiations with Akintola's camp, 85, 104
>   on Balewa's leadership, 33
>   British authorities and, 3, 14, 53
>   Coker Inquiry and, xxxiv, 84–85, 95, 97, 98–99, 100, 101–2, 104–6, 107–8, 149
>   comparison to Kano, 51–52

on decolonization, 1–2, 3, 10, 143
on development and economic nationalism, 13–14, 57, 62, 147
Farm Settlement Scheme and, xxvi, 59–60, 61, 64, 65, 74, 82, 147–48
federalism and, 10
on foreign aid, investment, and relations, 13–14, 17, 20, 24, 27, 53, 65
on Israel, xxv
Israeli relations, 3, 12, 13, 14, 53, 125–26
Israeli special assistance to Action Group and, 20–24, 27, 37, 52, 147, 148
joint corporations and, 24, 25, 26, 27, 52, 54–56, 91
legacy and reputation, 3, 22, 145–46
Macpherson Constitution and, 7–8
Path to Freedom, 2
political demise, 135
political philosophy and strategy, xi–xii, xviii, 22
progressive values, 61, 64
Rewane and, 175n66
rivalry with Azikiwe and Sardauna, 28, 30
social and economic programs, 12
treason charges, 105
Universal Primary Education program and, 69–70
See also Action Group

Western Region
introduction, xxxiii
Action Group leadership crisis and, 86–90, 91
investments in social and economic programs, 12
Israeli relations, 12–14, 41, 111, 117, 125–26, 147
joint corporations and, 24–25, 26–27, 52–56, 90–91
Macpherson Constitution and, 7
Richards Constitution and, 6
riots following Adelabu's death, 20
seats in federal House of Representatives, 29
self-rule, 8
shipping line negotiations and, 14–18, 19–20
state of emergency, xxxiv, 83–84, 90, 91, 93, 95, 135, 149
tensions with other regions, 8–9
Universal Primary Education program, 61, 69–70
See also Action Group; Awolowo, Obafemi; Coker Commission of Inquiry; Farm Settlement Scheme

For all types of unclear text structures (extensive, complicated, or undiscussed metatopic, or multiple, interweaving elements), the hierarchy of information is still a useful starting point to identify the different components of the book and how they fit together. The goal remains the same: to provide multiple access points to information throughout the index, and to still have a logical progression through the different levels of information. When indexing a more challenging book, remember that the different elements are all still present, even if the index structure needs to adapt. Let the book be your guide.

MULTIPLE ACCESS POINTS

Providing multiple access points is not, I admit, a type of structure. It is, however, very much about deciding where to place information within the index, and is part of indexing best practices. As such, it is important to keep in mind when building arrays and deciding how to piece the index together.

As the name suggests, providing multiple access points is about providing multiple places for readers to access the same information. The audience for a book can be a diverse group, and as indexers we need to try and anticipate the different ways in which they might search. Chances are, it is impossible to provide access points for all the different ways a reader might search, but it is often possible to anticipate the two or three, or more, most likely ways.

There are different methods for providing multiple access points. One is simply to provide entries for the different levels of the hierarchy of information, as I've previously discussed. One reader may search for a topic at a high level, such as the metatopic or a supermain discussion, while another may approach the topic through a more specific regular discussion or detail.

Another method is to provide cross-references from synonyms that may or may not be used in the text. For example, the text uses the name Myanmar for that Southeast Asian country. Anticipating that some readers may still search for the former name, you also include a cross-reference from Burma.

Double-posting is another way to create multiple access points, and can be used a few different ways. Instead of using a cross-reference from a synonym, in some cases it may be appropriate to double-post instead, with the same locators under both terms. For example,

> automobiles, 293, 301–302
> cars, 293, 301–302

Another way is to combine both terms together in a double-barreled term and flip the order, double-posting both versions. A double-barreled term is when two related, often synonymous, terms are combined, indicating that both terms are equally used in the text, and that readers will find one or the other on those pages:

> emotions and feelings, 232, 243, 265
> feelings and emotions, 232, 243, 265

Double-posting can also mean placing the same entry as both a main heading and as a subheading. One scenario is to gather similar terms into a single array, so that readers can either search for the specific term (standalone entry) or the broader term (larger array with subheadings). For example, double-posting museums and galleries at the University of British Columbia might look like this:

> Beaty Biodiversity Museum, 33, 35
> Morris and Helen Belkin Art Gallery, 29–31
> Museum of Anthropology (MOA), 34, 46–48
> University of British Columbia
>   Beaty Biodiversity Museum, 33, 35
>   Morris and Helen Belkin Art Gallery, 29–31
>   Museum of Anthropology (MOA), 34, 46–48

Another scenario is to only double-post information that can stand on its own. For example, say there is an extensive discussion about the astronomer Vera Rubin. Subheadings about specific aspects of her astronomy work, such as dark matter and the galaxy rotation problem, can be double-posted as main headings because these are clearly defined concepts within astronomy that readers might be interested in. Other subheadings, such as "background" and "legacy" should not be double-posted, since these describe something about Rubin rather than being independent concepts.

> dark matter, 45–47, 68, 99
> galaxy rotation problem, 30, 43–45
> Rubin, Vera
>   background, 42–43
>   dark matter and, 45–47, 68, 99
>   on galaxy rotation problem, 30, 43–45
>   legacy of, 47–49

If an array is too large to double-post, then use a cross-reference to redirect readers. Going back to the University of British Columbia example, say that the discussion about the Museum of Anthropology is so large that subheadings are needed to help readers find what they are looking for. Double-posting under the university is then no longer practical, and so a cross-reference from the university to the museum can be used instead.

When considering multiple access points, the goal is to place headings and subheadings where readers are likely to find them. Try seeing the information from the audience's perspective. Also remember that information often exists within a relationship. Try to find those places where information intersects, and then create access points for each facet of that relationship.

TAKEAWAYS

- Structure is about finding a home for every entry and array. The structure should enable readers to easily use and search the index.

- The table of contents approach to structure is to base the index on the structure of the book. This works best if the book's structure is clearly discernable.

- When the book's structure is less clear, still look for the hierarchy of information within the book. It should be present, even if it takes a bit more work to uncover. In the index, make sure that there are arrays corresponding to each level of the hierarchy of information, and that navigation between arrays is clear.

- Providing multiple access points to information is part of indexing best practices. Creating multiple ways to find the same information better serves a variety of users who may search differently.

TRY THIS

Examine the indexes you are studying as examples.

- How would you describe the index structure? Depending on the index, no discernible structure may be an appropriate answer.
- Can you identify a metatopic array? Supermain arrays? Arrays for regular discussions? How do these arrays relate to each other?
- Can you find multiple access points?
- Are cross-references used to redirect readers? Do the cross-references meet your expectations?
- If the index lacks a clear structure, how does that impact the user experience? How might the index be structured differently?

Think about your index.

- What is the text's structure, and can that be replicated in the index?
- If you tried the mind-mapping exercise from the previous chapter, think about the relationships between the metatopic, supermain discussions, and regular discussions. How can these relationships be expressed in the index?
- Is a simpler structure sufficient and appropriate, or should the structure be a little more complex? If more complex, what are some ideas that might work?
- Can you think of some examples of information for which you can provide multiple access points?

Keep in mind that you do not need to make a final decision now about structure. You will have a chance to revise the index, and I often continue to refine, or even change, the structure while editing the index. However, I also find it helpful to write the rough draft of the index with a structure in mind. At this point, try sketching out a rough plan for what the index might look like, and know that you can always change it later.

5

Format: Laying the Ground Rules

UP TO NOW, THIS BOOK has focused on the different components of an index and how to select terms and structure an index. This chapter will focus on the format.

Formatting considerations are important for ensuring consistency within the index and across all indexes. There are, however, a few variations to be aware of. For your own index, it is always a good idea to check with the publisher for their formatting guidelines. If the publisher does not have much of an opinion, or if the index is for a self-published book, then you will have to make your own decisions. Make those formatting decisions now, before starting the index, so that the format in the rough draft will be fairly clean. It may be a lot of work to go back and change the format later, so lay the ground rules now.

In this chapter, I primarily follow the *Chicago Manual of Style*, the standard in North America. Much of the discussion in this chapter should still be relevant if you live elsewhere in the world or are indexing a book for a publisher outside of North America. Just be sure to double-check the local conventions or publisher's guidelines.

In the end, regardless of the format you use, the most important element is consistency. If readers can trust that they understand the rules governing the index, then they will be able to search knowing that entries and arrays will be where they expect.

LAYOUT

The layout is how the index is designed and typeset. It is the index's visual appearance, and affects how easily, or not, the reader can scan and locate entries.

The two approaches are indented and run-in. Sometimes, as mentioned in the following section on sub-subheadings, it may be advantageous to combine both approaches, but in most cases, choose one or the other.

Check with your publisher to see whether they have a preference. If choosing yourself, consider the amount of space available for the index and the usability for your audience.

Indented Format

In indented format, headings and subheadings are stacked on top of each other. Subheadings are indented to indicate their relationship—that they are under—the main heading. Lines that run over onto two or more lines, such as the list of cross-references in the example below, should be further indented, to keep the distinction between lines clear.

With arrays spread out across multiple lines, this format is easier to read. It also takes up more space, especially if there are a lot of subheadings, so it may not be suitable if space is limited. Indented format is often used in cookbooks, reference books, children's books, and some trade books and textbooks. It is less common in scholarly books.

The following example is from *An Introduction to the Crusades*, by S.J. Allen. The first three arrays, for Isabella I of Castile, Isabella of Jerusalem, and Islam do not have subheadings and do not need to be indented. They are simply stacked on top of each other. The array for Islamic States does have subheadings, and all the subheadings, along with the cross-references, are indented.

Isabella I of Castile (r. 1474–1504), 45, 46
Isabella of Jerusalem (r. 1190–1205), 28
Islam, 6

Islamic States
   armies, 80
   arms and armor, 84–85
   background, 5–8
   economy, 7
   eleventh century, pre-crusades, 9–10
   First Crusade, views on, 17, 21–22
   fragmented nature of, 17, 19, 22, 23
   Holy Land, occupation by Fatimids, 9–10
   Jerusalem, significance for, 6, 108
   Jews and Christians in, 7–8, 44
   leadership, 6
   military strategy and tactics manuals, 87–88
   Second Crusade, unification after, 27–28
   social and cultural developments, 7
   Third Crusade, impact on, 32
   See also Ayyubid dynasty; Fatimid dynasty; Islamic world; jihad; Mamluk Sultanate; Ottomans; Seljuk Turks
   Israel, 134. *See also* Jewish communities

In addition to ease of reading, layout can also affect how subheadings are phrased. In indented format, try to lead with the key term so that the subject of each subheading is aligned on the left. This allows readers to more easily scan the list. In the example above, some of the subheadings, including "First Crusade," "Holy Land," and "Jerusalem," all include an additional phrase to clarify the focus of the subheading, while leading with the subject.

Cross-references can be gathered at the end of the array, on their own line after the subheadings. If no subheadings, then the cross-references directly follow the locators.

Indented format requires less punctuation. If no subheadings, then commas are used to separate locators from the main heading and from each other. Cross-references follow the locators on the same line, preceded by a period, with no closing punctuation. If subheadings, then commas separate locators from subheadings as well as each other. Semicolons separate cross-references from each other. Periods are not necessary.

Run-in Format

In run-in format, as its name implies, all the elements of the array run together, instead of being split onto separate lines. If the array requires more than one line, subsequent lines are indented, to distinguish arrays from each other.

Run-in format's principal virtue is that it is space efficient, especially if there are a lot of subheadings. Its downside is that it can be more difficult to read. Indexes for scholarly books often use run-in format, as indexes can be long with a lot of detail, and space for the index can be at a premium. Some trade publishers also prefer or allow run-in format. Sometimes, if the publisher does not have a strong preference and it seems like both might fit, I will submit the index in both formats and let the publisher decide which fits best.

Like indented format, run-in format can also affect how subheadings are phrased. Continue to try and lead with the key term, so that the subject of the subheading is the first term that the reader sees as they scan the array. However, it is also important that the subheading read naturally. With the subheadings packed together so tightly, inverting subheadings can break up the flow, as well as add more punctuation to an array that is already quite cluttered. Finding the right wording is a balancing act between readability and allowing key terms to pop out. Be aware of how the subheadings fit together, and of how the array reads as a whole.

Beginning subheadings with prepositions, which link back to the main heading, can also be a good way to create flow within the array. In the example below, from *The Collectors: A History of the Royal British Columbia Museum and Archives*, by Patricia Roy, I include the following subheadings after "field work": "for displays in new buildings," "by historians," and "with UBC."

Field Museum, 16, 17, 26, 384
Field Trippers program, 503n70
field work: Brooks Peninsula Refugium Project, 432–33; for displays in new building, 194, 197; explanation of, 414; by historians, 417; Indigenous collection, 51, 118; interdisciplinary research trips, 432, 433, 443; marine

biology, 123–24, 420; mice population study, 126; natural history, 19, 56, 57, 97–98, 354–55, 431, 442–43; PEACE project, 443–44; with UBC, 125. See also *Living Landscapes* program
Fifth Pacific Science Congress, 65
film: in archive's collection, 258–59, 270; educational films by museum, *110*, 111–12

In run-in format, cross-references follow locators and/or subheadings, on the same line.

For punctuation, arrays with no subheadings are as normal, with a comma to separate locators from the main heading and from other locators. With subheadings, punctuation becomes more complicated, to clearly differentiate between the different parts. A colon is used to separate the main heading and the subheadings. Commas are used between subheadings and locators. Semicolons are used to separate subheadings from each other. For cross-references, a period is used to separate the cross-reference from the rest of the array, with semicolons again used to separate specific cross-references from each other. There is no period at the end of arrays.

There are a couple of related techniques—sub-subheadings and the em-dash-modified format—that can be used to shape the index. These are especially handy for arrays with a lot of subheadings that resist easy organization.

SUB-SUBHEADINGS

Sub-subheadings, as the name implies, is a third level of headings, after main headings and subheadings. These provide options for breaking down a discussion even further. Say, for example, an array for Zambia contains a subheading for "history." If there is extensive discussion about Zambian history, say more than ten locators, or if there is a long page range, then sub-subheadings may be helpful for breaking that discussion down into smaller, more accessible, chunks of information.

There are pitfalls to using sub-subheadings, however, and I rarely use them. Many of my trade and scholarly clients explicitly request that sub-subheadings not be used, though they are more common in certain disciplines, such as medicine. If you are considering using them, check with the publisher first, or review indexes in related books to see whether this is an accepted technique within that discipline.

One pitfall is the temptation to be too specific, beyond what is necessary or useful. In most cases, a handful of locators can be contained within a single subheading; each locator does not need its own individual sub-subheading. Only use sub-subheadings when there are too many locators for readers to reasonably search or if the additional clarity benefits readers.

Another pitfall is that sub-subheadings can make the array difficult to read. For example, here is an array on sustainable businesses, first in indented format and then run-in format.

sustainable businesses
    advantages of, 66-67, 117, 134-135
    business models for, 68–70, 118–119
    certifications and standards
        B Corporation, 72–73, 144, 150-152
        EU Ecolabel, 83–84
        Fairtrade, 76–78
        Rainforest Alliance, 74–75, 91
    circular economy and, 78, 155–156
    as green capitalism, 43–45, 122, 188–189
    vs. greenwashing
        in automobile industry, 54, 141–142
        consumer impacts, 150–151
        definition, 139
        by political actors, 146–148
    principles of, 34–36
    triple bottom line, 178–179

sustainable businesses: advantages of, 66-67, 117, 134-135; business models for, 68–70, 118–119; certifications and standards: B Corporation, 72–73, 144, 150-152; EU Ecolabel, 83–84; Fairtrade, 76–78; Rainforest Alliance, 74–75, 91; circular economy and, 78, 155–156; as green capitalism, 43–45, 122, 188–189; vs. greenwashing: in automobile industry, 54, 141–142; consumer impacts, 150–151; definition, 139; by political actors, 146–148; principles of, 34–36; triple bottom line, 178–179

The indented version of this array is still readable. The main consideration is to make sure that the indents are clearly visible so readers can track the different levels of headings. The additional indents for the sub-subheadings also shorten those lines, making it more likely for lines to run over, which could substantially lengthen the array and be challenging to read.

The run-in version, in contrast, is much more difficult to follow. The sub-subheadings blend in, making it appear that the subheadings are out of alphabetical order. You could try tinkering with the punctuation, or perhaps add some bold or other styling, to help the sub-subheadings stand out (I show an example in the next section), but otherwise run-in format for sub-subheadings should be avoided.

As a compromise solution, designed to be both compact and readable, the *Chicago Manual of Style* suggests combining both indented and run-in formats. The subheadings are indented, and the sub-subheadings are run-in.

> sustainable businesses
>   advantages of, 66–67, 117, 134–135
>   business models for, 68–70, 118–119
>   certifications and standards: B Corporation, 72–73, 144, 150-152; EU Ecolabel, 83–84; Fairtrade, 76–78; Rainforest Alliance, 74–75, 91
>   circular economy and, 78, 155–156
>   as green capitalism, 43–45, 122, 188–189
>   vs. greenwashing: in automobile industry, 54, 141–142; consumer impacts, 150–151; definition, 139; by political actors, 146–148
>   principles of, 34–36
>   triple bottom line, 178–179

These layout and readability problems are amplified if more than three levels of headings are used. In theory, it is possible to use as many levels of sub-subheadings as you would like, but only use more than three if it is an accepted convention within the discipline you are working within, and if alternative options are not working. In most cases, keep it simple and stick to just main headings and subheadings, especially if the index is in run-in format. Readers may not notice the punctuation that indicates the change in level and may instead complain that the subheadings are out of alphabetical order.

There are a few options to avoid using sub-subheadings while keeping a high level of specificity. One is to hive off the subheading to form its own main entry, with a cross-reference from the original array. For example, in the sustainable businesses array above, I could turn "certificates and standards" and "greenwashing" into their own arrays with subheadings.

Another option is to create parallel subheadings. Say, for example, in a chapter on food production, there is extensive discussion about how food is distributed, and it would be helpful for the reader to see the different methods clearly distinguished. Sub-subheadings can be used, with "distribution" as the subheading and "rail," "ship," and "truck" as the sub-subheadings. Or, the sub-subheadings can be converted into three separate subheadings, eliminating the need for a third level.

> food production
>   distribution by rail
>   distribution by ship
>   distribution by truck
>   employment
>   environmental impacts
>   genetic diversity and seed security
>   severe weather and

In this scenario, I try to avoid more than three stacked subheadings (stacked meaning that the subheadings begin with the same words). Too many, and eyes may start to skip over. On the other hand, beginning with the same phrasing—"distribution by"—keeps these subheadings sorted together, so that readers easily see all three methods. If the subheadings are instead written as "rail distribution," "ship distribution," and "truck distribution," then they may be interspersed with other subheadings and are more likely to be overlooked. This option also works best if there are only a few potential sub-subheadings. If more than three distribution methods were discussed, for example, I would probably instead create a separate array, for food distribution, treating these as two distinct, though related, topics.

A third option to sidestep sub-subheadings is to create a series of main headings all beginning with the same term. I discuss this in the next section on the em-dash-modified format.

My one exception to using sub-subheadings is for listing works by an artist or author. Consider this example from *Blowing Up the Skirt of History: Recovered and Reanimated Plays by Early Canadian Women Dramatists, 1876–1920*, by Kym Bird. The following array is in both indented and run-in formats (the index was submitted in run-in format).

Carter-Broun, Louise
    acting and movie career, 242–3, 245, 249n5, 250n18
    background, 242, 248n2
    death, 245, 249n8
    as feminist icon, 248
    Haswell and, 243–4, 249n9
    lack of acquaintances with other women writers, 17
    photographs, *13, 243, 247*
    playwriting, 43, 243, 244, 245
    plays by
        The Awakening, 245
        Bedfellows, 244
        Cherie, 245
        Clouds, 244
        The Joy of Living, 244
        Teddy's Marriage, 245
    See also *The Soldiers* (Carter-Broun)

Carter-Broun, Louise: acting and movie career, 242–3, 245, 249n5, 250n18; background, 242, 248n2; death, 245, 249n8; as feminist icon, 248; Haswell and, 243–4, 249n9; lack of acquaintances with other women writers, 17; photographs, *13, 243, 247*; playwriting, 43, 243, 244, 245; plays by: *The Awakening*, 245; *Bedfellows*, 244; *Cherie*, 245; *Clouds*, 244; *The Joy of Living*, 244; *Teddy's Marriage*, 245. See also *The Soldiers* (Carter-Broun)

This is the array for one of the profiled playwrights, Louise Carter-Broun. The first set of subheadings details the playwright's life and career.

The second set is a list of plays, followed by a cross-reference to the primary play that the book discusses with its own array with subheadings.

The plays are all listed as sub-subheadings. I could have placed them as subheadings, but they would then be interspersed among the biographical subheadings, which visually is much messier. In this instance, the third level creates a separation between the two types of information, while keeping them together in one array. Also note that the subheading "plays" is force-sorted to the end, as technically "playwriting" should be last. In arrays like this, I always force-sort so that the array has two distinct parts. It also helps that the plays are in italics, which, especially in run-in format, provides an additional visual cue.

EM-DASH-MODIFIED FORMAT

As I mentioned in the previous section, one technique for sidestepping sub-subheadings is to create a series of main headings, all beginning with the same term. Put another way, the subheading is run back to join the main heading, collapsing three levels into two. This is called the em-dash-modified format (or simply the modified format, if without the em dash):

>   Edmonton
>   festivals
>   Cariwest
>   Deep Freeze
>   parks
>   Hawrelak Park
>   Mill Creek Ravine

becomes

>   Edmonton, festivals
>   Cariwest
>   Deep Freeze
>   Edmonton, parks
>   Hawrelak Park
>   Mill Creek Ravine

This is one of my favorite methods for structuring enormous, complicated arrays, such as when a person is the metatopic. While one option is to create multiple, smaller arrays scattered throughout the index, breaking up certain subjects feels wrong. I will discuss the em-dash-modified format in the context of three examples: for books about artists and writers, for biographies and memoirs, and for history.

I occasionally have the opportunity to index a critical assessment of an artist or writer. These books often include biographical details, perhaps other indexable details about their career or how they created their works, and extensive discussions and mentions of specific works. The works alone can form very long lists, and I use the em-dash-modified format to help categorize and sort.

I did this for the collection *An Echo in the Mountains: Al Purdy After a Century*, edited by Nicholas Bradley, which provides new critical perspectives on the Canadian poet Al Purdy. To make the array more accessible, and especially Purdy's works, I created the following entries:

> Purdy, Al: approach to, 4–5, 6–7, 26–9; against academia, 223–5; appeal of, 4; …
> —ANTHOLOGIES: *Fifteen Winds*, 254, 259n9, 259n12; *Storm Warning*, 259n9; *Storm Warning 2*, 31n16, 259n9
> —POEMS: "After the Rats," 12, 32n20; "After Yeats' Lapis Lazuli," 226; "Alive or Not," 60; …
> —POETRY COLLECTIONS: *Being Alive*, 15, 183, 184; *The Blur in Between*, 31n12, 32n20, 34n34, 49, 164n7; *The Cariboo Horses*, 8, 31n12, 91, 158, 191, 248; …
> —PROSE: "Arctic Poems and Prose," 109, 115, 119; *Cougar Hunter*, 150; *Morning and It's Summer*, 197, 205–6, 208, 209, 210, 213; …

Technically, this is a series of five separate arrays. The first, for "Purdy, Al," contains all the subheadings for Purdy's life and career. It is a large array, but still short enough that I thought a single array was sufficient.

The following four arrays are for the various types of work that Purdy produced: anthologies, poems, poetry collections, and prose. These are all subheadings that I ran back. The em dash replaces Purdy's name, indicating that these are separate from, yet still related to the initial main heading. The types of works are also placed in all caps, or small caps, as an additional visual cue to readers to help distinguish between the arrays.

Each array also contains subheadings. To give a sense for how this looks on the page, I have included the first three subheadings for each array, in run-in format. The shortest array is for anthologies, with only three subheadings. The longest array is for poems, with just over two hundred poems listed. That is enormous, but it works because I have pre-sorted the works so that only poems are included. A reader looking for a specific poem only needs to search in one location.

This series of arrays also works because the categories are broad. I could have tried to subdivide further. For example, instead of prose I could have included arrays for autobiography, essays, fiction, and letters. Or maybe I could have tried to organize the poems by year or by significant periods in Purdy's life. But that would also require more work on the reader's part, trying to decide which of the narrower categories is relevant for their search, as well as creating a longer list of arrays to scan. When using the em-dash-modified format, keep it simple. Its overall effect should be to simplify.

Biographies and memoirs are also about the life of a single person, with each chapter devoted to a separate aspect of that life. One option is to create separate arrays for each of those parts, with cross-references from the person's name, but as I mentioned above, it feels unnatural to me to scatter a person's life like that. A person's life is a unified whole, even if the components that make up that life are diverse.

Ujjal Dosanjh is a retired Canadian politician. He immigrated to Canada from India, became a lawyer, was a cabinet minister at both the provincial and federal levels of government, and was premier of British Columbia. In his retirement, he wrote his memoir, *Life After Midnight*.

To keep all the entries together for the metatopic array, I created the following modified arrays, shown with their first three subheadings.

Dosanjh, Ujjal: appetite of, 72; on dealing with idiots, 89; on emigration, 170; ...

Dosanjh, Ujjal, as BC attorney general: and Aboriginal rights, 338-39; and Air India investigation, 350; appointment to, 321-22; ...

Dosanjh, Ujjal, in BC provincial politics: 1979 Vancouver South NDP nomination, 193-95, 197-98; 1979 Vancouver South NDP campaign, 199-200; 1983 Vancouver South campaign, 207-8, *276, 277*; ...

Dosanjh, Ujjal, childhood and early adulthood: at Billayhana farm, 10-11, 12; buffalo incident, 31; and buffalo milk, 43; ...

Dosanjh, Ujjal, education: application to study in England, 58-61; application to UBC, 148; at Bahowal School, 20, 21-22; ...

Dosanjh, Ujjal, in England: application to study in, 58-61; arrival in, 80-82; caste system in, 100; ...

Dosanjh, Ujjal, family life: and 1986 election, 269-70; and Bob and Leah Osterhout misunderstandings, 162; and election campaigns, 191; ...

Dosanjh, Ujjal, in federal politics: 1974 election, 191; 2004 election campaign in Vancouver South, 411-12; 2006 election campaign, 424; ...

Dosanjh, Ujjal, law career: after 1979 election, 201-2; articling, 164; call to bar, 167; ...

Dosanjh, Ujjal, political involvement: and 1980 Vancouver mayoral election, 202; and Attorney General office, 152; and B.C. Human Rights Branch, 152; ...

Dosanjh, Ujjal, and Sikh/Indian politics: altercation at Ross Street Temple, 130-31, 132-33; column in *Link,* 231, 236-37; false assault charge against, 160-61; ...

Dosanjh, Ujjal, trips to India: 1994 trade mission trip, 317-18; and Air India bombing, 255-56; in Amritsar, 175, 176, 214, 264, 394; ...

Dosanjh, Ujjal, in Vancouver: arrival in, 118; back injury, 129, 132, 133, 135, 231-32; first job at lumber mill, 119; ...

Dosanjh government: 2001-02 budget, 398-99; achievements of, 397, 398-99; and balanced budget bill, 381-82; ...

This is a book I indexed earlier in my career. Looking back at it now, I wince a bit at the sheer number of arrays—fourteen! Yet I am also hard pressed to think how I would streamline it today. Dosanjh accomplished a lot, and trying to keep all the elements together yet distinct was a challenge.

Notice that I did not use em dashes. I simply ran back what would have been the subheadings, and kept Ujjal Dosanjh's name at the beginning of all the main headings. I also did not use all caps or small caps.

I cannot remember now why I made this decision to repeat Dosanjh's name, but I want to include this example as an alternative formatting option.

In my experience, scholarly authors and publishers understand the function of the em dash. For trade books, I once had an author (not for this book) request that I change it because they found the em dash confusing, though other trade clients seem fine with it. When deciding which format to use, consider, and maybe consult, your audience.

The first array, for "Dosanjh, Ujjal," functions as a catchall, for subheadings that do not fit anywhere else.

Also notice that some of the main headings are very specific—"BC attorney general," "Sikh/Indian politics," "trips to India"—while others are more general—"BC provincial politics," "federal politics," "political involvement." This reflects both the contours of Dosanjh's career and what he chose to focus on in his memoir. For example, there was far more discussion about his time as the BC attorney general than his time as the federal health minister, which meant that the discussion for BC attorney general required subheadings whereas his time as health minister made more sense as a subheading itself under "federal politics." Deciding appropriate entries is a matter of paying attention to the text, seeing what is important, and seeing what can be grouped together.

Let's shift now from people-centered books. The em-dash-modified format can also be useful for sorting and simplifying complicated arrays in other contexts, in this next case, history.

This example is from *Canada's Army*, 3rd edition, by J.L. Granatstein. The book is a history of the Canadian army, covering its iterations since its inception and its involvement in various wars as well as peacekeeping and peace-time endeavors. There was a lot of detail to pick up, including specific military units and battles. I used the em-dash-modified format extensively to try to make the arrays as user-friendly as possible.

Let's start with the arrays for the Boer War, which was a relatively minor discussion in the book.

Boer War, 33–42; arrival in South Africa, 36; Canadian complaints, 37, 39; Canadian reforms following, 42–3; deaths from disease, 98; enemy engagement, 37–9, 40, 41–2; equipment, 36; Hughes and, 51; jingoist attitudes and Canada's commitment to, 33–5; medical care, 40; mobilization, 35–6, 39, 42; Nursing Sisters, 35, 383; return to Canada, 40–1, 42; South African constabulary, 42
—BATTLES: Boschbult, 42; Israel's Poort, 40; Leliefontein, 41–2; Paardeberg, 37–9; Wolve Spruit, 41
—MILITARY UNITS: 2nd (Special Service) Battalion, Royal Canadian Regiment, 35–9; 3rd (Special Service) Battalion, Royal Canadian Regiment, 39; Canadian Mounted Rifles, 39, 41, 42; "F" Company, 35; "G" Company, 38; "H" Company, 38; Lord Strathcona's Horse, 39, 41, 42; Royal Canadian Dragoons, 41–2; Royal Canadian Field Artillery, 39, 41, 42

The first array gathers all the descriptive information about the Boer War that the book discusses. The second and third arrays gather specific battles and military units. Combined, these point toward everything that the reader might want to know. The em-dash-modified format both holds it all together while also allowing for a clear separation between the parts.

The em-dash-modified format was also useful for wars with much larger discussions and much more complicated arrays. Below are two sets of arrays for the Great War (First World War).

The first is for the Canadian Expeditionary Force (CEF), the field force that Canada put together as their contribution. This follows the overall structure I used for the Boer War, as I tried to keep the structure similar throughout the index. The first part gathers various aspects for how the CEF operated and fought.

The second part is for all the formations and divisions. This was the most complicated part of the structure and the one that I spent a lot of time trying to figure out. Because there were so many units mentioned and discussed, I decided to combine the em-dash-modified format with sub-subheadings. The first level of subheadings are the types of units: divisions, brigades, battalions, Canadian Mounted Rifles, and specialist units. To make these easier to see, I used bold to highlight them. I also force-sorted these subheadings to follow the military's hierarchical ranking, which I thought appropriate for a military history, and perhaps easier to read for military buffs than alphabetical sort. The sub-subheadings are all the specific units.

Looking closer, some of the units, such as most of the divisions, had enough locators to merit subheadings of their own. Instead of a fourth level of headings, which seemed a level of complexity too far, I gave these units their own arrays and included cross-references so that readers who start their search here will be redirected to the right place. (Also note that the cross-references are incorrectly formatted. According to the *Chicago Manual of Style*, cross-references from subheadings should use a lowercase *see* and *see also*. I was so focused on figuring out the structure that I forgot that detail, though in the end, I don't think it matters too much.)

Under battalions, I also included a general cross-reference to "other unnumbered battalions." I still have mixed feelings about that, as it requires readers to know the names of those unnumbered battalions. If I could go back, I would probably include the names with a cross-reference to their main array. At the time, however, the array already seemed enormous; I was feeling pressure from the deadline; many of the unnumbered battalions appear in other wars and contexts too, which would have added an additional task of figuring out which locators belong here and which do not; and I was already struggling with figuring out a structure that both included all the details while still being easy to use. For better or worse, this is what I settled on.

> Canadian Expeditionary Force (CEF): arrival in Britain, 58–9; casualties, 148–9; conscription, 118–22; demobilization and repatriation, 80, 156–7, 158–9; education initiatives, 126; French Canadians, 54, 69–70, 94, 121, 150; home defence duty, 81, 118–19; Hughes and, 52–3, 56, 69, 71–3 (*See also* Hughes, Sam); Kinmel Camp riot, 157–8; leadership, 56, 69, 72–3, 88–9; officer selection, 55–6; Permanent Force and, 56; recruitment, 52–5, 67, 68–71, 72, 474n65; training, 57–8, 75; venereal disease, 80; war graves, 161, 486nn29; weapons and equipment, 51, 57, 63, 87. *See also* Canadian Corps (WWI)

—FORMATIONS AND UNITS: **divisions**: First Division (*See* First Canadian Division (WWI)); Second Division (*See* Second Canadian Division (WWI)); Third Division (*See* Third Canadian Division (WWI)); Fourth Division (*See* Fourth Canadian Division (WWI)); Fifth Division, 120, 122–3, 149, 479n63; **brigades**: 1st Brigade, 55, 60, 62, 64, 75, 130; 2nd Brigade, 55, 60, 64, 65, 74, 75, 76, 92; 3rd Brigade, 55, 60, 62, 64, 74; 4th Brigade, 55, 67, 73; 5th Brigade, 67, 94; 6th Brigade, 67, 86; 7th Brigade, 84, 94, 95, 143, 145, 156; 8th Brigade, 84–5; 9th Brigade, 84, 121, 148; 10th Brigade, 110; 11th Brigade, 109–10, 479n56; 12th Brigade, 109, 110; Canadian Cavalry Brigade, 59, 74–5, 123–4, 133; Engineer Brigade, 129–30; Motor Machine Gun brigades, 57, 127; **battalions** (*See also* other unnumbered battalions); 1st Battalion, 62, 66, 75, 109, 148; 2nd Battalion, 64, 133, 166 (*See also* Hastings and Prince Edward Regiment); 3rd Battalion, 64; 4th Battalion, 62; 5th Battalion, 118; 7th Battalion, 54, 63, 64–5, 87, 114; 8th Battalion, 54–5, 62–3, 114; 10th Battalion, 59, 65, 71, 132, 154–5; 10th Reserve Battalion, 71; 14th Battalion, 74; 15th Battalion, 62–3; 16th Battalion, 108, 138–9, 166 (*See also* Canadian Scottish Regiment); 18th Battalion, 139, 140; 20th Battalion, 137; 21st Battalion, 94, 114; 21st Reserve Battalion, 71; 22nd (Van Doos) Battalion, 67, 69, 71, 85, 94, 121, 137 (*See also* Le Royal 22e Régiment); 25th Battalion, 94; 26th Battalion, 94; 27th Battalion, 82, 99, 131; 28th Battalion, 86; 29th Battalion, 114, 155; 31st Battalion, 71, 93; 41st Battalion, 71; 42nd Battalion, 80, 84, 126, 143; 43rd Battalion, 84, 144; 44th Battalion, 110, 114, 138; 46th Battalion, 117, 134–5, 484n185; 49th Battalion, 71, 84, 86, 95, 117; 50th Battalion, 71, 110; 52nd Battalion, 84; 54th Battalion, 110; 57th Battalion, 71; 58th Battalion, 84, 93; 60th Battalion, 84, 121; 61st Battalion, 93; 69th Battalion, 71; 75th Battalion, 134; 85th Battalion (Nova Scotia Highlanders), 110, 120, 139; 91st Battalion, 71; 116th Battalion, 121, 143–4; 150th Battalion, 71; 163rd Battalion, 71; 178th Battalion, 71; 189th Battalion, 71; 227th Battalion, 68; 258th Battalion, 71; **Canadian Mounted Rifles**: 1st Canadian Mounted Rifles, 84, 120; 2nd Canadian Mounted Rifles, 84, 109; 4th Canadian Mounted Rifles, 84, 134, 484n176; 5th Canadian Mounted Rifles, 84, 95, 132; **specialist units**: 1st Canadian Tunneling Company, 82; 2nd (Coloured) Canadian Construction Company (No. 2 Construction Battalion), 157, 473n56; Canadian Army Dental Corps, 97; Canadian Army Medical Corps, 97, 98, 99; Canadian Army Service Corps, 56, 77, 101, 154; Nursing Sisters, 97, 98 (*See also* Nursing Sisters)

The one set of details not included in these arrays are the battles. Nor does the initial CEF array contain details about the Great War as a whole. There was so much going on in the CEF array that I decided to have separate arrays specifically for the Great War. This included the battles, separated from the initial descriptive subheadings using the em-dash-modified format.

> Great War, 50–150; overview, 59–60, 115, 135, 146; Armistice, 148, 153; attrition, 92–3, 106, 115; burial of dead, 98, 101, 160–1, 486n29; Canada's entry, 50; Canada's forgetfulness of, 151–2, 160; Canadian nationalism and, 123, 141, 150, 152; comparison to WWII, 183, 203; conscription, 118–22; gas warfare, 60, 62–3, 75, 96, 114, 127; German retreat, 146–8; map of Western Front, xix; medical care, 63, 96–9, 138; memorials, 160; Rhineland occupation, 153–6; shell shock, 99–100, 130; tanks, 93, 94, 136; trenches, 60, 61, 73–4, 76–7, 78–9, 104; unified Allied command, 124; US entry, 110, 115, 119. *See also* Canadian Corps (WWI); Canadian Expeditionary Force
> —BATTLES: Amiens, 130, 131–5, 140; Arras, 106; Artois (1915), 73–4; Cambrai (1917), 123–4; Cambrai (1918), 146; Canal du Nord, 141–6; Drocourt-Quéant Line, 135–9, 140; Festubert, 74–5; Givenchy (1915), 75; Hill 70, 113–15; Hill 145, 107, 109–10; Mons, 148; Mont Houy, 147; Moreuil Wood, 124; Mount Sorrel, 84–5, 86–7, 91; Neuve Chapelle, 60; Passchendaele, xxiv, 115–18, 480n88; Somme (1916), 92–3, 103; Somme (1918), 135; St Eloi, 82–3, 99; Valenciennes, 147; Verdun, 82, 92, 93; Vimy Ridge, xxii–xxiii, 106–11, 130; Ypres (1915), xx–xxi, 60–6, 91, 473n44

Combined, these arrays cover all aspects of the Great War and the Canadian Expeditionary Force. With so much information to cover, I decided to split the information up between the two different arrays—one for the war itself and one for the Canadian army. The em-dash-modified format (and sub-subheadings) allowed me to further organize the arrays, separating out the details for the battles and military units. With extensive cross-references to all the other military units also involved, readers should be able to quickly find the specific information they are looking for.

As a final note, the *Canada's Army* example is probably a much more complicated structure than you need. In my own work, that index is the only time so far that I have ever combined sub-subheadings with the em-dash-modified format. I offer the example, though, to show what is possible.

For your own index, there is a good chance that you will not need to use the em-dash-modified format. Keep the index structure simple. Only make it more complicated if two levels—headings and subheadings—do not seem enough. If the arrays you are working with do become too large, complicated, and difficult to navigate, then the em-dash-modified format is a great option to make it simple again.

SORTING

Once the information in the book has been deconstructed and structured into arrays, the arrays need to be placed in the index. But how and where?

Sorting according to the hierarchy of information is too subjective. It may make sense to you, as the indexer, but it may not be immediately obvious to readers. This means time spent searching and possibly not finding the information they want. A neutral standard is needed, one that can be applied to all indexes. Sorting according to the alphabet has become the default solution.

Alphabetical Sorting

There are two types of alphabetical sort, letter-by-letter and word-by-word. The difference can be subtle. Whichever you use—whether following the publisher's style guide or your own choice—be consistent.

As its name suggests, letter-by-letter sorting is focused on the letter. Spaces between words are ignored. Alphabetization continues until the first comma or parenthesis, after which it begins again.

For word-by-word sorting, the key unit is the word. In addition to stopping at the first comma or parenthesis, alphabetization also stops and begins again at the end of each word. This can be helpful for grouping together several people with the same surname, who might otherwise have their names interspersed among other entries.

In my experience, in North America, letter-by-letter sorting is more common, though always check with the publisher. If you live outside of North America, or are indexing in a different language, you may want to ask around to see if the convention is different for your particular context.

In the following example, the two different sorting approaches affect a few entries: daikon; Dai Li; diadem; DiLisi, Francesca; and Di Mauro, Luca. It has not affected others: *Daily Mail*, daylight, dimples, and the main headings beginning with Denton. This is likely the case for most indexes—many entries will sort the same either way, and readers may not notice the difference, so long as entries remain close to where readers expect. It is part of best practices, though, to be consistent.

Letter-by-Letter	Word-by-Word
daikon	Dai Li
Dai Li	daikon
Daily Mail	*Daily Mail*
daylight	daylight
Denton (NC)	Denton (NC)
Denton (TX)	Denton (TX)
Denton, Zahara	Denton, Zahara
Denton Township (MI)	Denton Township (MI)
diadem	Di Mauro, Luca
DiLisi, Francesca	diadem
Di Mauro, Luca	DiLisi, Francesca
dimples	dimples

Articles, Conjunctions, and Prepositions

As important as alphabetical sort is, there are a few exceptions. The key to these exceptions is that they complement alphabetical sort and facilitate a more intuitive user experience.

The first exception is that articles, conjunctions, and prepositions are generally ignored. When sorting, the focus is on the first significant term.

Articles—*a*, *an*, and *the*—indicate things (a cat, the floor). Conjunctions, such as *and* and *but*, connect clauses and sentences, with *and* being the most common used in indexes. Prepositions allow for relationships to be more precisely expressed. Common prepositions in indexes are *on, in, by, for, of,* and *versus*.

Articles, conjunctions, and prepositions affect sorting at both the main heading and subheading levels. Consider these examples from *Open to Think*, by Dan Pontefract.

> purpose, clarity about, 189, 193–94
> *The Purpose Effect* (Pontefract), 11, 57, 73, 189
> purposeful procrastination, 96–97
> ...
> Rilke, Rainer Maria, 30
> "The Road Not Taken" (Frost), 1–4, 5
> Ruiz, Karyn, 37–38, 63, 88, 115, 144, 171, 200–201, 226–28
> ...
> time
>   common thieves of, 134–35
>   for Critical Thinking, 133–37, 144
>   decision-making and time of day, 54
>   exploitation vs. exploration of, 66–67, 68, 82
>   management of, 190, 201, 220
>   outsourcing, 136
>   realism, 137
>   for reflection, 49, 50, 52, 62–64
>   scheduling, 61, 70–72, 88, 89
>   situational capacity, 136
>   technology constraints, 94–95

At the main heading level, *The Purpose Effect*, a previous book by Pontefract, and "The Road Not Taken," a poem by Robert Frost, are sorted as if "The" is not there. I chose to simply ignore the article; some publishers and indexers prefer to either invert such titles or simply leave the article out, for example, *Purpose Effect, The* (Pontefract) or "Road Not Taken" (Frost). Before deciding on an approach, first check with the publisher.

Ignoring the article typically applies to all creative works and or proper nouns, including place names, though the *Chicago Manual of Style* notes an exception for titles and place names in non-English languages, for audiences not familiar with the non-English articles. For these, such as *Eine, El, La,* or *Los,* sort on the article.

At the main heading level, also note that only articles are ignored. Titles beginning with a preposition, such as *On the Banks of Plum Creek* (Wilder) or *Of Mice and Men* (Steinbeck), are still sorted on the preposition.

At the subheading level, though, prepositions and conjunctions, along with articles, are all ignored. Articles, conjunctions, and prepositions can be placed at either the beginning or the end of subheadings. If at the end, then they will probably not be a factor for sorting, as in the "common thieves of" and "management of" subheadings in the "time" example above. In some cases, though, it makes more sense to place them at the beginning of the subheading, as in "for Critical Thinking" and "for reflection." Placing the preposition at the front, in these examples, more clearly expresses the relationship between the main heading and the subheading, as well as has a more natural flow when read. For sorting, the *for* is ignored and the subheading is sorted according to the key term.

When should conjunctions and prepositions be used in subheadings? Both are used to express a relationship between the subheading and main heading, though sometimes, as in "outsourcing" and "scheduling," in the example above, the relationship can be implied. If the relationship is potentially unclear, however, it is best to clarify. *And* is very common, and indicates some sort of relationship without being specific. In some cases, if it is either not important to provide further detail or if the relationship is complicated—too complicated to detail the nuances in the subheading—then *and* is an excellent choice. In other cases, prepositions can be a simple way to provide a little more information for how the two terms intersect.

Generally, when sorting main headings, ignore articles. When sorting subheadings, ignore articles, conjunctions, and prepositions. Occasionally, such as when indexing non-English titles and names, exceptions should be made. If you think this might be your situation, consult the *Chicago Manual of Style*, or whichever style guide you are following.

Chronological and Page Order Sort

Sometimes (such as in indexes for biography and memoirs), chronological or page order sort is used instead of alphabetical sort. Main headings are still sorted alphabetically. Only subheadings may be sorted chronologically, and usually only for the subject of the biography or memoir—who will often have a very long array. The rationale is that lives unfold as a series of events. By ordering the subheadings according to time, a mini-narrative unfolds, which can be delightful to read.

The difference between chronological and page order sort is that in chronological sort, the placement of subheadings is deliberate to conform to the chronology. Page order sort means that subheadings are arranged according to when they first appear in the text; if the text is written chronologically, then the subheadings should naturally be chronological as well.

Page order sort, however, does not work with every book. Biographies and memoirs may be structured thematically, or may begin with a splashy introduction before settling into the narrative, which interferes with the order in the index. Page order and chronological sort may also both run into the problem that some elements of a life are not chronological. Friendships, hobbies, and political and religious beliefs, for example, may contain milestones that exist in time, yet are also things that can follow a person throughout a life, and it can be difficult to pinpoint where, in the chronology, it belongs. Chronological sort also works well if the reader is content to browse or if the reader knows where, roughly, in the chronology to search, but less well if the reader is looking for a specific subheading. Lacking the objective structure imposed by alphabetical sort, the reader may have to read the entire array to find what they are looking for, which takes time.

I rarely use chronological sort, and have never used page order sort. I find it too subjective and potentially too confusing and difficult for readers to find specific entries within the array. I like the clarity and standardization that alphabetical sort provides. It is also possible, working within alphabetical sort, to massage how subheadings are phrased, which can lend itself to a mini-narrative while still sorting alphabetically. That said, if you are interested in a fuller and more positive endorsement of chronological and page order sort, as well as discussion of some of the cons, see Hazel Bell's excellent book, *Indexing Biographies & Other Stories of Human Lives*.

The one time I did use a chronological sort, I only applied it to the em-dash-modified main headings. This was for *The Ocean's Whistleblower: The Remarkable Life and Work of Daniel Pauly*, by David Grémillet. Daniel Pauly is a marine biologist and environmental activist, focused on global fisheries. As I often do for biographies, I used the em-dash-modified format to break up the metatopic array into more manageable chunks. I also realized that the five em-dash-modified arrays that I decided to use naturally formed a chronology, flowing from Pauly's childhood to career. Combined with the first three subheadings for each array, it looked like this (trigger warning: Pauly had a difficult childhood):

> Pauly, Daniel: about, 314; absentmindedness, 117-18, 133-34; Canadian citizenship, 308; …
> —CHILDHOOD: abuse and neglect from foster family, 7-8, 9-10, 14, 17; attempts to run away, 10; birth and early childhood, 3-4; …
> —YOUTH: employment in France, 28; employment in Germany, 20-22; French mandatory military service, 25-26, 27-28, 66; …
> —EDUCATION: baccalaureate studies and exam, 21, 22-23, 29, 31, *165*; doctoral program, 71-72, 73-75, 76-78; Ghana research trip, 55-58; …
> —CAREER: 1980s pace and scope of work, 132-33, *171*; Africa and, 263, 264, 282; arrival and departure from ICLARM, 84-85, 86, *167*, 188-89; …
> —WORKS: overview, *182*, 308; *Darwin's Fishes,* 245-46; "Fishing Down Marine Food Webs," *176*, 206-10, 211-17; …

This chronology provides that sense of a mini-narrative while still being simple enough for readers to quickly scan and pinpoint which array they want to dig deeper in. It works because it is subtle and reflects a natural life progression—hopefully subtle enough that readers accept it without being confused. I also only used it because the em-dash-modified arrays lent themselves to a chronological order, rather than trying to force the arrays to fit.

For the nitty-gritty details of the subheadings, though, under each em-dash-modified array, I still used alphabetical sort, to be consistent with the rest of the index and with what readers are probably expecting.

I do not use page order sort. I think it leaves too much to chance, to assume that the book will be written in a way that will naturally unfold nicely in the index.

I realize that it is easy to find an example of page order sort used poorly, and that the counterargument is that I did not look hard enough to find an example in which it worked well. However, I think it is useful to know what to avoid. The following example is from *God's Funeral*, by A.N. Wilson, which is described as a "synthesis of biography and intellectual history" about the loss of religious faith in the nineteenth century. Page order sort is used throughout the index, for all the subheadings. But because the book is focused on multiple people and is more a history of ideas rather than events, the result, as seen in the array below for David Hume, is more a mishmash of random subheadings than a coherent chronology. For ease of reading, I have placed the array in indented format, instead of the original run-in format.

Hume, David
    religious scepticism, 9–10, 22–5, 29–30, 46, 51, 180, 326
    on immortality, 26
    influence on Morley, 26–7
    style, 28
    influence on Kant, 33–4
    influence on Bentham, 42
    Carlyle on, 60
    Pusey reads, 107
    Newman reads, 115
    Jowett reads, 120
    Green recommends abandoning, 123

and race memory, 157
empiricism, 158
Spencer and, 165
and design in nature, 188, 352
and sensations, 315

I suppose if readers were already familiar with the book and the intellectual history, then this order might make sense. For the uninitiated, a reader would need to read the entire array to find what they want, because there is no way to anticipate where in the array the sought-for subheading will fall. I think alphabetical sort would be much clearer and easier to use.

Force-Sorting

Force-sorting is when the alphabetical order is deliberately changed. If using indexing software that automates the alphabetical sort, this means overriding the software's settings. If alphabetizing manually, then force-sorting simply means deciding to sort a particular entry differently.

I have already discussed examples of force-sorting. Ignoring articles, conjunctions, and prepositions, in order to sort on the key term or the first significant word, is force-sorting, and one that indexing software programs are set up to do automatically. Chronological or page order sort will usually require force-sorting, since it is only a subset of entries—usually just subheadings, and maybe just for one or two arrays—which need to sort differently. Placing a subheading for introductory material at the top of the array may also require force-sorting.

Force-sorting can also be used to make small adjustments to how main headings are sorted. I use this sometimes when there is a long list of similar entries, and I do not want the starting point to be buried. Say, for example, there are several main entries for different aspects about cats. Instead of making these aspects subheadings under "cats" (the discussions are too large and each aspect needs their own subheadings), and instead of using the em-dash-modified format, I have decided to simply use a series of main headings. The problem, though, is that "cats," under both letter-by-letter and word-by-word sorting, will sort near the bottom of the list.

I think it makes more sense, however, to have the most general of the main headings at the top. So, I force-sort "cats" to the top and end up with the following main headings:

Letter-by-Letter	Word-by-Word	Force-Sorted
cat breeds	cat breeds	cats
cat evolution	cat evolution	cat breeds
cat food	cat food	cat evolution
cat health	cat health	cat food
cats	cat socialisation	cat health
cat socialization	cats	cat socialisation

Books with extensive discussions of a particular family, both the family as a whole as well as specific family members, are also good candidates for force-sorting. I often force-sort the array for the family to the top of the list, in front of the individual members. This way, readers can first get a sense of the family as a whole, and the family array is not overlooked. I did this for *Strangers in the House*, by Candace Savage, about the Blondin family, in which there are twenty-nine people with the Blondin surname:

Blondin (Sureau dit Blondin) family
Blondin, Adéline (née Trottier; wife of Augustin Blondin)
Blondin, Alexandre Sureau dit
Blondin, Alice
Blondin, Allelina Sureau dit
Blondin, Antoinette Sureau dit
Blondin, Antoinette (Nettie) Sureau dit
...

Use force-sorting sparingly. It works best for small adjustments that improve usability within an array or a small subset of similar arrays. Do not try to make major structural changes to the index. When done well, the tweak should feel intuitive, and readers should be able to easily use the index without noticing the change.

NUMBERS AND SYMBOLS

Numbers and symbols pose a problem in alphabetical sort because they are clearly outside of the alphabet. Yet some terms do begin with a number or symbol, and symbols may themselves be the topic of discussion.

There are two approaches to sorting these or you can double-post.

One approach is to sort the term as if spelled out. For example, 49th Parallel Coffee Roasters would be sorted as if spelled forty-nine. Greek letters used in mathematics or science would be sorted according to how they are spelled in English. This works well when there are only a handful of such entries.

The second approach is to place these entries at the beginning of the index, before the As. This works best when there are several arrays of the same type. For example, a book on computer programming may discuss specific symbols used in coding. Or, a military history may discuss specific military units, such as the 4th Division or 18th Battalion, and it may be helpful for readers, in order to see which military units are discussed, to see all the units together.

If numbers are sorted together, either as main headings at the beginning of the index or as subheadings at the top of the array, numbers are sorted in numerical order. This also applies to regnal numbers. For example, the popes Leo VIII, Leo IX, and Leo X. Entries beginning with dates, alternatively, might be better sorted chronologically.

If you are interested in more information, Nancy Mulvany goes into greater detail in her book *Indexing Books*.

CAPITALIZATION

An old convention called for all the main headings to be capitalized, and you can still occasionally see this in some indexes. However, it is much more common today to only capitalize proper nouns.

Another way to think of this is, follow the text. If the term is capitalized in the book, then capitalize in the index. If not, then index

> ### How Often Can the Rules Be Broken?
>
> Not very often.
>
> Indexing conventions are important for training readers how to use an index and for reassuring readers that the indexes they encounter will function as expected. Doing something drastically different can pull a user out of the index, and make them question their ability to use the index or whether the information they are searching for exists.
>
> That said, indexes also need to be appropriately organized to match the contents and structure of the text. Sometimes it is necessary to bend or break a rule in order to make an index work.
>
> Some examples of breaking or bending the rules include force-sorting, using unruly or long strings of undifferentiated locators, or raising or lowering the bar for what is counted as a passing mention. Reasons for breaking the rules could be to better showcase the subject matter, or maybe space for the index is tight and you are trying to cram in as many entries as possible.
>
> If you do decide to bend the rules, try to keep the changes small. Think carefully about why the rule is not working and why the change might improve the user's experience. Ideally, readers will not even notice because they will more easily be able to find the information they are looking for.

the term as lowercase. You can also check with the publisher for their preference.

In subheadings, only proper nouns are capitalized.

TAKEAWAYS

- In contrast to structure, which is about how the information within the index is organized, format is about the formal rules and conventions that govern how the different elements of the index are organized and presented.

- Layout refers to the visual presentation of the index. Indexes typically use either indented or run-in format. Indented format is easier to read, while run-in format is more space efficient.
- Sub-subheadings are a third level of headings that allow a topic to be broken down even more granularly. However, sub-subheadings can also make the array more difficult to read and not all publishers accept them.
- The em-dash-modified format is an alternative to sub-subheadings, through creating a series of stacked arrays. It works by keeping entries for large discussions together, while also subdividing the entries into smaller chunks, which are easier for readers to scan.
- Alphabetical sort refers to ordering arrays and subheadings alphabetically. It is a neutral, widely accepted standard, allowing readers to confidently navigate any index. Alphabetical sort can be either letter-by-letter or word-by-word.
- Within alphabetical sort, certain common words—typically articles, conjunctions, and prepositions—are usually ignored, with sorting based on the first significant word in the term or phrase.
- Chronological and page order sort are alternatives to alphabetical sort. Deliberately breaking alphabetical sort is also called force-sorting. However, deviating from alphabetical sort can make the index more difficult to use, as the new system may not be immediately obvious to users. Changes to alphabetical sort should only be done carefully and sparingly, in a way that appears natural for that context.
- Numbers and symbols can be placed either at the beginning of the index or sorted as if spelled out.

- Only capitalize proper nouns.
- Be consistent.

TRY THIS

Look through your stack of example indexes:

- What is the usability like for indented versus run-in format?
- Do the subheadings follow alphabetical, chronological, or page order sort? If you are able to find examples of chronological or page order sort, how does that choice affect the user experience?
- How are conjunctions and prepositions used?
- Are you able to find examples of force-sorting?
- Are there entries beginning with a number or symbol? How are they sorted?
- How are main headings capitalized?

Think about the index you are writing:

- If the book is being published by a traditional or hybrid publisher, have you checked to see whether the publisher has guidelines for indexing?
- If you are making the formatting decisions, do it early on so that you can format correctly as you write the rough draft. Consider: indented or run-in format, letter-by-letter or word-by-word sorting, whether or not to use a different sorting method than alphabetical, how to handle numbers and symbols, capitalization, punctuation, and locator ranges.

6

Five-Step Framework for Indexing

EVERY INDEXER INDEXES DIFFERENTLY. SOME like to work from a hard copy of the page proofs, while others prefer to read from a PDF. Some read the book once, while others make multiple passes. Some like to mark up the text as they read, while others do not. There is no right or wrong approach.

In this chapter, I discuss a five-step framework for writing an index. All indexers, one way or another, go through these stages. I also offer suggestions for how each stage can be put into action. In addition, I offer some thoughts on layout and typesetting, indexing from a list of terms, and updating an index.

As you read this chapter, think about how you like to work. Does one approach or another feel right? Feel free to experiment and to mix and match. Also, be open to your indexing process changing over time as your skills and confidence improves. I know my process has.

There will be a learning curve as you become familiar with the steps and put together your own process. Your first index, or first few, may be among the most difficult that you will write. And that is okay. Indexing will get easier with practice.

STEP 1: GET READY

For me, writing an index often feels like running a marathon. Some indexes are quicker and easier than others, but even the fast, short indexes require at least two days to write. I need a plan. Once I start an index, I am in it for the long haul. While I know that reaching the finish line is eminently possible, I also know that I need to settle in and take my time. Sprinting will only leave me exhausted, and the index worse off.

As you sit down to begin writing your index, take a moment to review what you have so far and to make sure you have the right tools in place.

- The book or document. Make sure that you have a complete copy. If you are indexing from a PDF, make sure that the layout is final, so that the page numbers are fixed, or at least final enough that major changes are not anticipated. (Finding and fixing a final few typos in the manuscript should not disrupt the index. If the layout does change, and the index needs to be updated after it is written, see page 112.) If you are writing an embedded index (in which tags are inserted into the text), then the layout and page numbers will not be an issue.

- Double-check and familiarize yourself with the formatting guidelines, whether from the publisher or the ones you have decided on. If you have not yet thought about format and layout, take a moment now to make those decisions. While it is possible to change your mind partway through, it can be time-consuming and finicky to go back and make changes to the whole index. As much as possible, implement the format you want from the start. Format considerations to decide include the following:
    - indented or run-in format
    - letter-by-letter or word-by-word alphabetical sorting
    - main headings capitalized or just proper nouns

- locator formatting, including abbreviation of ranges and indication of figures, tables, and notes
- other special elements, such as sorting terms beginning with numerals

- Make note of how much space is being reserved for the index. If you are not sure, check with the publisher. Some publishers allow as much space as is necessary, while others may have a limit for how many pages or lines can be included. The amount of space for the index can also sometimes be negotiated. Having a clear sense for how long the index can be is important because if space is limited, you may need to make decisions about what to include in the index and what has to be left out. See page 146 for more details on fitting a tight space.

- Gather and review any thoughts and notes you may have for the index. Do you have an idea for what the metatopic is? What some of the supermain and regular discussions might be? How the book is structured? What kind of structure might be suitable for the index? Who the audience is, and what they might need in the index? Any ideas and insights you bring to the index, whether extensive or light (I do not always know a lot about the book when I start), will guide your work, as well as be further refined as you dig into the details of the text and index.

- Decide how you will create the index. Will you use software specifically created for indexing? Will you type out the index in a word processor? Use index cards? All these options will result in an index. Some methods are more labor intensive, while others will require time to learn and possibly money to buy. I discuss these options in more detail on page 99. Think about what best suits your needs and goals right now.

- Create a place to keep notes. This can be a separate Word document, a notes app, or a piece of paper. I find it helpful to have an external brain, so to speak, to dump ideas as I index and to keep track of typos and other notes to myself.

- Block out time in your schedule. Plan for at least a week, possibly a month, depending on how long your book is and how much time you can dedicate each day or week. Keep in mind that indexing is intellectual labor and you may only be able to index three to five hours at a time or per day. Remember to make time for both writing the rough draft and for editing the index. It may also be helpful to break the work into smaller chunks, such as indexing a chapter or a certain number of pages per day. For more thoughts on time and planning your schedule, see page 11.

- Get comfortable. Brew a pot of tea or coffee. Find a time and place to work without interruptions and distractions. It is time to focus and get to work.

STEP 2: READ THE TEXT

The second step is to read the text.

Read the text with an eye toward indexing, even if you wrote the book or have previously read the book.

Books contain a lot of detail. While you may be able to sketch an accurate outline from memory, it is best to (re-)read the book and index what is on the page, rather than from your memory. Your prior knowledge will still be useful for anticipating how the book is structured, and what terms and discussions will be important, but to ensure accuracy and that all relevant details and discussions are included in the index, (re-)read the text.

The second reason for reading the text is because reading to index is different from reading for pleasure, or for research, or for editing and proofreading. Reading to index is an active process. It is determining the aboutness of a specific portion of the text, considering how it fits into the

Three Methods for Getting the Index Down on the Page

Writing an index is an intellectual task, requiring constant decision making. At some point, entries also need to somehow get onto the page, and a rough draft needs to be written. There are different ways to do this. Most professional indexers use specialized software, which might be an option for you too. There are also more manual methods, either using index cards or a word processor.

There is no right or wrong method, so long as an index is written. Some of these methods are more labor intensive, while others have a greater learning curve and may cost money to buy the necessary tools. Here, I briefly outline the manual methods, as well as software. As you prepare to index, think about how you might want to start. If you decide to index more often or professionally, you can also always change your method.

Indexing with Index Cards

I have never written an index using index cards. I have listened to long-time and retired indexers describe the process. It sounds labor intensive and laborious. Software is an immense improvement, allowing the indexer to focus more on creating entries and building the structure, and less on the mechanics of formatting and sorting. However, if you prefer a more tactile experience with paper and pencil, or want to take a break from the computer, or just want to try indexing old school, this method may be worth trying.

Nancy Mulvany details the process in *Indexing Books*, on pages 246–248. In essence, the process is as follows:

- Write one entry per card. An entry is a main heading, subheading (if needed), and a single locator. For subheadings, it may be easier to add them to most entries, just in case, and then edit them out later, rather than having to go back to add. Also, remember that a cross-reference can also be a locator.

- Stack cards, as they are created, in page order. Once a stack accumulates, check page numbers (or other locators) for accuracy, and then alphabetize cards and place in a container. Many long-time indexers talk about using shoe boxes.
- Once cards have been made for the whole book (a whole draft written), it is time to edit. Spread the cards out so that entries can be seen and compared. Rearrange, add, remove, and make corrections as needed. When done, re-alphabetize.
- Type all the edited entries into a word-processor file, using the correct format.

Indexing with a Word Processor

When I say indexing with a word processor, I simply mean typing the entries into a word processor. I do not mean using the embedded indexing function in Word, or automated alphabetization, or any other special functions that have a learning curve and that may or may not be suitable for indexing. The goal, here, is to keep the indexing process simple.

Start by opening a blank document. Type the first entry: main heading, locator, maybe a subheading. Then type the second entry, and keep going until the whole book is indexed. Once you have a complete rough draft, it is time to edit and proofread the index.

As you type the entries, also alphabetically sort and format the entries. While sorting and formatting as the entries are created can be slow, I think it is easier and faster than typing the entries in page order and then having to sort and format hundreds, if not thousands, of entries at the end.

This is how I learned to index, and how I wrote the first dozen or so indexes I ever wrote. I like it because it is simple. I did not need to learn any new software (to be honest, I also did not know yet that indexing software existed), and having to figure out the sorting and formatting myself helped to engrain the mechanics of an index. The downside is that it is labor intensive and will require more proofreading to ensure that the format and alphabetical sort is accurate.

Despite its drawbacks, this is the method I recommend if you are trying out indexing or only planning on writing one or two indexes. It is cheap, will help ground you in the mechanics of indexing, and allows you to start right away.

Indexing with Specialized Software

Specialized indexing software can be an immense help. The value, for me, is that it automates the formatting. That alone saves time and eliminates mistakes that I may introduce or overlook. Software also makes it easier to edit and manipulate the index. For example, in the program I use, Cindex, I often create a subgroup of entries if I want to focus on editing a small portion and temporarily ignore the rest. I can also label entries with different colors, which helps me keep track of which entries are completed and which still need revising.

It is important to remember, though, that there is no software that will write the index for you. There is software that promises to do just that, using algorithms to select terms. But the result is almost always unsatisfactory, often producing an unedited list of terms lacking structure and subheadings. Extensive editing will be required to make it usable. It is better to make your own decisions, and to only use software as an aid.

Indexing software also requires time to learn, and most programs cost money to buy, though there are some free or trial options. If you decide to index regularly or professionally, then this cost in time and money quickly becomes worthwhile. If you are only writing one or two indexes, then maybe not.

If you are interested in learning more about software, I outline the main options on page 186. I also list some options for embedded indexing on page 188.

larger context of the chapter or book, whether it is relevant to the audience, and then thinking about how to translate that into main headings and subheadings. Reading to index is a constant process of analysis and synthesis. Different questions are asked of the text than when reading for pleasure or research. Editing and proofreading are also an active engagement with the text, but these are tasks that ask different questions and have different goals. While you may find typos while indexing (I often do), if you are both indexing and proofreading, I suggest keeping these tasks separate.

STEP 3: WRITE THE ROUGH DRAFT

The third step is to write the rough draft through creating the index entries.

This step overlaps with reading the text. Simply saying "write the rough draft" is also a bit of a simplification, as there are a few steps involved, depending on the approach you choose. However, I think it is important to differentiate these two steps to emphasize that reading the book, with an eye toward indexing, is important. Drafting the index is, then, taking what you have read and turning it into index entries.

The first approach to writing the rough draft is to start with marking up the text. As you read, highlight, scribble, underline, circle: whatever works for you to start extracting potential entries. This can be done on a hard copy or on a PDF. Items to note could include names of people and organizations, places, concepts, things, dates, figures and tables, and any other information of note. Think about what pieces of information might be the metatopic, or a supermain or regular discussion, or something more minor yet still indexable. Include notes for potential subheadings and cross-references. At this point, you are getting to know the text through the prism of indexing. There are no right or wrong decisions. You can always change your mind later.

Once the text is marked up—you can either mark up the whole book or work chapter-by-chapter—go through all the notes and type them up as entries. On this second pass, evaluate what you have marked. Having read the whole book, some potential entries may no longer seem relevant, while other subjects may need to be fleshed out with more subheadings, if they prove more important than you originally thought. Having gotten familiar with the book's structure, it may also be easier figuring out how to arrange the entries into an appropriate structure. You can also get a sense for how many entries are being picked up per page, which may tell you if you are overindexing or underindexing.

Once the second pass, to type the entries, is finished, you should have a complete rough draft.

The second approach is to pick up and create the index entries as you read the text. In this process, you are reading, analyzing, determining what might be indexable, and then, instead of marking the text, are deciding on the spot and adding the entry to the rough draft.

For example, say I start reading a chapter, which I see is on referendums in British Columbia. Reading further, I see that there are discussions about the 2018 electoral reform referendum and on the 2011 Harmonized Sales Tax (HST) referendum. Realizing that these should be double-posted and have subheadings—at least in the rough draft—I create the following entries:

> British Columbia
>   electoral reform referendum (2018)
>   Harmonized Sales Tax (HST) referendum (2011)
> electoral reform
>   British Columbia referendum on
> Harmonized Sales Tax (HST)
>   British Columbia referendum on
> referendums
>   electoral reform (2018)
>   Harmonized Sales Tax (HST; 2011)
> taxes
>   Harmonized Sales Tax (HST) referendum in British Columbia (2011)

Later, when I edit the index, I might choose to revise these entries. I may remove subheadings if the array remains small without additional

How Many Entries Do I Need to Pick Up Per Page?

The short answer is, as many entries as is necessary.

Nancy Mulvany, in *Indexing Books*, suggests that trade books will usually average three to five entries per page, while reference books, textbooks, cookbooks, medical texts, and scholarly books will have six to eight entries per page. Other documents, such as policies and procedures, manuals, and technical documentation, may have eight or more entries per page.

I generally agree with Mulvany. It is also important to understand where these numbers are coming from and how it applies to specific books.

Audience, and how the audience will use the book and index, is one factor. Readers of a trade book are often more comfortable with a lighter index, while readers using the book for research or as a reference will want a more detailed index, as the index will be the main point of entry.

It is also important to pay attention to the type of book or text. Biographies and history, for example, will often contain a lot of names, most of which, if not all, should be indexed, and which will take up a lot of space. Business books, in contrast, are much more focused on concepts, and will have far fewer names, resulting in fewer entries. A policy document may average ten policies per page, and each policy will need one to three entries, taking into account double-posting, which could easily mean more than twenty entries per page, which is appropriate for that index.

Space for the index is also an important factor. The less space there is, the fewer entries will fit.

I wish I could give you an easy answer. Each book and index will be different. You will need to take into consideration what is indexable and how much of it there is, along with audience expectations and how much space is available for the index.

> Mulvany's suggestions can still be helpful as guidelines, though. If you notice that you are picking up more than eight entries per page for a trade book, or only averaging three entries per page for a scholarly book, ask yourself why. It may indeed be appropriate for the text, or it may mean that you are either overindexing or underindexing. Also remember that these numbers are an average per page. Some pages may have fewer, even just one entry, while others may have more.

information; or, I might revise main headings, for example, electoral reform becomes electoral reform referendums; or, to use acronyms (BC and/or HST) at the subheading level instead of spelling out the whole phrase; or, I may change how and where I use the dates; or, I may use a cross-reference from British Columbia to referendums instead of double-posting. It depends on what other entries I pick up for these arrays and how much space I have to work with. But, for now, these entries clearly label what the information is, they provide multiple access points, and I feel confident enough to move on with creating the rest of the rough draft.

To make this second approach easier, first review the table of contents to see what the chapters are about. It may also be worth skimming ahead in the chapter to see what the section headings are, or to first read the introductions and/or conclusions for both the book and each chapter. This will give you ideas for the supermain and regular discussions, which will become main entries in the index.

Both approaches work well and have their adherents. There are some professional indexers, with decades of experience, who continue to mark up the text before creating the rough draft. Other indexers like to dive right in and build the draft as they read. It comes down to personal preference and working styles.

If you are just learning how to index, I suggest starting with marking up the text. This provides time and space to think about potential entries before committing them to the page. Having a chance to reconsider entries, on the second pass while writing the draft, may also mean a cleaner draft, which will be easier to edit. This I how I learned how to index, and it was only after three or four years of marking up the text that I switched to drafting on the fly.

Also remember that the index is, at this point, rough. It does not need to be perfect. The goal is to get your first thoughts and impressions onto the page, where they can be edited later.

STEP 4: EDIT THE INDEX

Once the rough draft is written, the index needs to be edited.

I like to give myself some time between writing the rough draft and editing. In practice, this usually means finishing the rough draft one day and starting to edit the next. I find the break helps me to see the index with fresh eyes.

When planning your schedule, expect to take at least a couple of days to edit the index, possibly as long as it took to write the rough draft. You will be reviewing every entry for accuracy and clarity and making sure that the index structure holds together.

Start with reviewing the format guidelines. Part of editing is making sure that the format is correct. It is also a good idea to refresh your memory of the main discussions and book structure, to regain a big-picture view of the book after having focused on the details while drafting. I like to create either a new mind map or write a brief summary of the book. This can help you assess how well the index reflects the book and how best to edit the index structure.

There are a couple of different approaches to editing. One is to start from the top (or from the bottom) and systematically edit every entry. The goal is to finish an entry, move on, and not return and edit a second time, though I still sometimes change my mind or notice an error and have to go back.

Alternatively, some indexers like to make multiple passes. One pass could be to edit the headings and subheadings for clarity and relevance.

Another pass may be to edit the structure. Another could be to check cross-references, and another could be to proofread for spelling and punctuation, for example. Begin by making a list of editing tasks, and then decide how you want to break that up.

When finished, some indexers like to put the index aside for a day, and then do one, final pass, with fresh eyes, to pick up any last awkward phrasing or formatting and spelling errors.

If you are using indexing software, the program should handle the formatting, and you will not need to spend as much time checking that. If you are using a more manual approach, then you will need to carefully proofread the index, in addition to editing for clarity and structure. When proofreading, check that the alphabetical sort is correct, that the locators are in the correct order, and that the correct layout and format has been used.

There are many aspects of the index to check, ranging from the big picture to the minutia. Here is a list of things to look for:

- What is the metatopic and is there a clear metatopic entry or entries?
- Do the supermain discussions have entries? Is the relationship between metatopic and supermains clear?
- Do regular discussions have entries? Is the relationship between supermain and regular arrays clear?
- Does the index have a discernible structure?
- Does the index accurately reflect the book? Are topics missing from the index, or are there entries which should be removed?
- Are entries relevant for the audience?
- Are main headings and subheadings clearly worded? Do the relationships between main headings and subheadings make sense? Is bias present in how headings and subheadings are phrased?
- Are subheadings necessary and relevant? Should subheadings be added, combined, or removed?

- Are cross-references accurate and used where needed?
- Are multiple access points provided, whether through double-posting or cross-references?
- Are names properly spelled and inverted?
- Are locators accurate and in the correct order, including locators with special formatting, such as for figures, tables, or notes?
- Are there long strings of undifferentiated locators? Do these arrays need subheadings?
- Is the alphabetical sort correct?
- Is punctuation correct?
- Is spelling correct?
- Is a headnote necessary to explain any special features?

If the index proves too long for the space allotted, this is also the time to trim the index. I provide some tips on page 146.

STEP 5: SOLICIT FEEDBACK

The last step I recommend, especially if you are new to indexing, is to solicit feedback. It can be easy to index in a way that makes sense to us, as the indexers, but ultimately the index needs to work for readers.

For professional indexers, this usually means sending the index to the author or to the publisher, who may ask for revisions. Another possibility, especially if you are indexing your own book, is to find beta readers. You can also try the Index Peer Review email group.

When asking for feedback, ask questions like, What are their first impressions? Are headings and subheadings clearly written? Is navigating the index easy or difficult? Are they able to find the topics they expect to find? Do they feel inspired and confident to use the index again?

Depending on the feedback, you may need to revise. This can be an unwelcome chore after all the work you have already done. I encourage

> ### Editing the Metatopic Array
>
> Indexing the metatopic can be tough. Technically, everything in the book is indexable under the metatopic, yet that is clearly not practical. This is why separate arrays are created for the supermain and regular discussions.
>
> Still, it can be difficult to know what to include in the metatopic array. Should the array serve as a summary for the whole book, with long ranges for each of the supermain discussions? Should the array be a clearinghouse, using cross-references to redirect readers? Should the array contain background information, which does not fit anywhere else?
>
> When I am unsure about how to handle the metatopic, I often edit the metatopic array last. This allows me to first clearly see how all the other topics are handled. Once I know what the supermain and regular arrays look like, it is often easier to see how the metatopic array fits into and can serve the overall structure.

you to still assess the feedback and make at least a few changes. Your index, and your book, will be better for it.

When the index is completely done, submit the final draft to the publisher (or to the author to forward to the publisher, depending on who you are working with). If you are self-publishing, the index can now be typeset.

LAYOUT AND TYPESETTING

Once the index is finished, it is ready to be typeset. This is not part of the five steps, and, if you are working with a publisher, you may not need to do anything with the layout. However, I think this is still worth mentioning.

If working with a publisher, or if you are self-publishing and have hired a designer, give them the finalized index. Submit the index as a Word document or RTF file. Single column is fine. Arrays should be properly indented, using a hanging index. Otherwise, no special formatting is needed. Let the designer do their job.

If you are designing the layout yourself, you will need to make a few decisions. First, the number of columns. Most indexes are typeset in two columns, though indexes in large format books may have three or four columns. Columns should be wide enough to read comfortably, without causing too many words to break awkwardly. Font size can be a little smaller than the main text, though still readable. Arrays, for both run-in and indented format, should be properly indented. Some arrays may be interrupted by a page break. For these, a "(continued)" at the top of the next page may be helpful. The A, B, C, etc... headings at the beginning of each alphabetical section can be included or omitted, though there should be a space between sections.

Once the index is designed, give it a final proofread. If the index is being handled by the publisher, you can ask to review the proofs. Check that all the entries are present, that the alphabetical sections are properly separated, that the indentations are correct and arrays properly distinguished from each other, and that line breaks make sense and are readable. The purpose is to double-check the designer's work. As with anything, another pair of eyes is helpful. If you'd like, you can also do a final check for spelling and alphabetization.

INDEXING FROM A LIST OF TERMS

You may get advice, even from publishers, that the best way to index is to start with a list of terms. This might be a list that you write yourself. After the list is written, either you or someone else will search the text for these terms and add the page numbers.

I think the rationale is twofold. One, the indexing process can begin while the book is still being edited and typeset. Two, the assumption is that searching the text to find terms is the fastest way to index. Another assumption is that the index is simply a list.

But the result, more often than not, is an index that lacks thought. Instead of subheadings, arrays contain long strings of locators, some of questionable relevance. The index lacks a discernible structure. Main headings may be awkwardly phrased. Relevant discussions may be omitted because the search tool failed to find them.

The search tool also lacks context. Part of indexing is understanding which terms and discussions are relevant, and how terms and discussions relate to each other. This works best if you read the whole book. Relying on the search tool, in contrast, forces you to jump around the text, which makes it much more difficult to understand the context. Using the search tool will also require you to spend time weeding out irrelevant hits. From personal experience, relying on search can actually take a lot more time, and be much more frustrating.

Search is also an imperfect tool. I do use search when indexing, to gauge how often a term is mentioned (useful for deciding if an array needs subheadings), or to quickly find and double-check an entry when editing. But I am also aware of its limitations. Names are particularly tricky, as people may be referred to by their full name, a part of their name, or a pronoun or title. Words can also change, whether through conjugation, or from singular to plural, or simply a spelling error. Unless you specifically look for these variations, search will not pick them up. To ensure that you are finding all relevant discussions, read the book.

If you are concerned about choosing relevant terms for the index, or about the indexer (if someone else is writing the index) choosing relevant terms, try brainstorming a list of key terms as an alternative to writing an exhaustive list. Go through the hierarchy of information in the book and pull out possible terms for the metatopic, supermain discussions, and regular discussions. Do not worry about the smaller details, which you, or the indexer, will find as you read the text. Use this list as a reference to guide your work. But instead of using search, read the book. Create the index using the framework I have outlined. The resulting index will be better.

UPDATING AN INDEX

Occasionally an index needs to be updated. Something in the text has changed, and the index needs to be adjusted in order to be accurate again.

This usually happens because of one of two scenarios. The first is that a substantive change has occurred to the text or proofs shortly after the index has been written. Perhaps a paragraph has been added or removed, or a table has been moved from one page to another. This might result in a few entries having to be added, removed, or edited, but the main effect is reflow. Reflow is when the layout of the text shifts, so that the page numbers (or other locators) in the index are no longer accurate.

The second scenario is when a new edition of the book is being published, which may be several years after the previous edition. Similar to the first scenario, there is probably some material in the text that has been added, removed, or revised. The whole book may have also been redesigned, with a new layout and new page numbers.

The key question, when facing these scenarios, is, is it better to update the existing index or is it better to start from scratch? I find that a lot of publishers assume that updating the original index is faster and easier than writing a new index, but that is not always the case. Each book and index need to be individually assessed.

In the first scenario, I often update the existing index that I have already written. Changes to the entries themselves are usually minor, and the main issue is reflow. It also helps that the index is still fresh in my memory.

It is important to get a sense for how extensive the changes are. If working with a publisher, ask for a list of changes or for an annotated PDF with the changes marked. Sometimes only a single chapter is affected and updating the index can be done quickly, within an hour. Sometimes multiple chapters, or the entire book, is affected, and it can take a couple of days to check and update every locator.

When adjusting locators for reflow, compare the new, revised proofs with the proofs that you indexed from. Go through page by page, looking for places where the layout shifts. When you find such places, compare the revised proofs to the index, looking for the entries from that page, and adjust the locators, if necessary. If reflow is minor, chances are only a few locators will need to be updated, but the only way to be certain is to go through systematically.

If the index is for a new edition of the book, there are a few more factors to take into account. Start by assessing how extensive the changes are. If the changes are primarily due to reflow, updating the locators will still be tedious, but the process is straightforward. If extensive changes have been made to the text, then updating the index can become much more complicated. Now it is a matter of making sure that all relevant entries are added, removed, or revised, which could end up being a few hundred entries. All those changes to the text can also make reflow much more difficult to track. To make it easier to track the changes, ask the publisher for a list or annotated manuscript. Another question is, did you write the original index? If yes, it may be easier for you to make these changes, since you understand how the index was written, and may even remember writing it. If not, it can be quite difficult to get into the mind of the previous indexer and reverse engineer the original index, even for a well-written index, since every indexer thinks a little differently.

In many cases, when indexing a new edition, it is better to index from scratch. This is especially true if changes to the text are extensive and if the original index was written by someone else. I learned this the hard way with my very first freelance contract. The book was an edited volume, with a few chapters removed, added, and shuffled into a new order. The publisher blithely suggested that it would be easy to update the original index, and I, not knowing better, gave it a try. Updating the index was a nightmare, though I somehow made it work, and the publisher was happy enough with the result to hire me again. The saving grace, perhaps, is that I was not familiar with the subject matter, and so writing the index from scratch would have also been challenging. It taught me, though, to never assume that updating an index will be easy, and to always carefully assess.

MY INDEXING PROCESS

Indexing is a paradoxical craft. It is governed by rules and conventions, yet every indexer has their own unique process and will produce a unique index.

I want to briefly share my indexing process, as an example for how all these steps can fit together. I also want to emphasize that your process can be different. As you learn how to index, feel free to experiment with different approaches and be open to your process evolving as your skills and confidence increase. If something from my process makes sense, feel free to adopt it. If not, that is okay too. There are many ways to implement the five-step framework.

I like to start a new index by briefly reviewing the publisher's guidelines, reading the table of contents, and skimming ahead a few chapters. This helps orient me to the requirements for this particular project and begins to seed my mind with what the book is about, both the metatopic and supermain discussions. This also gives me a sense how long chapters are, whether chapters are split into sections, and whether there are a lot of illustrations or tables.

I then jump right in and start picking up entries for the rough draft as I read the book. For the first three or four years that I indexed, I marked up the text prior to creating the rough draft. I found that helpful because I was still learning how to read as an indexer and learning how to structure the index. Once these skills started to become habit, I decided that marking up the text was no longer necessary.

That said, indexing on the fly is not always easy. Sometimes I am confident that the entries I create will make it to the final draft. Other times I feel like I am just throwing entries onto the page, hoping that something will stick by the time I come around again to edit. If I get really stuck, I will read ahead a few pages until I understand the full discussion and then come back to create the entries. My goal is to pick up everything that seems relevant, while still filtering out passing mentions. My rationale is that it is easier to edit than to go back later to find what I missed, though I do sometimes have to go back. Usually, this process works well for me. Once I see all the potential entries together on the page and understand the larger context, the arrays start to make sense, and I can see how to edit.

Once the rough draft is finished, I like to give myself some space before I edit. This usually means sleeping on the index and starting to edit the next day. This clears my mind and helps me to see the index more objectively.

I start editing from the top of the index and work my way down. I try to finalize each array before I move on. I jump around a little if, for example, it makes sense to edit a cluster of arrays on the same topic. When finished, I label these arrays with a color code to indicate that they are done, so I do not edit them again, and then return to where I left off in my top-down approach.

When the whole index is edited, I do another quick pass to check cross-references. I also check the spelling. I then send the index to the client and wait to hear whether revisions are requested. If yes, sometimes revisions take just a few minutes, and usually no longer than an hour or two.

Once done, I usually have another index lined up to begin, and the whole process starts over.

TAKEAWAYS

- While all indexers follow their own unique process, all indexes are written according to a basic five-step framework.
    - Step 1: Get ready. This includes settling on an indexing process, making sure that all the necessary materials and tools are ready, creating or reviewing the formatting guidelines, and blocking time in your schedule to index.
    - Step 2: Read the text. Read with your indexing hat on, as opposed to your writing, editing, or pleasure-reading hat. Make sure you understand what the book is about.

- Step 3: Write the rough draft. Whether you pre-read and mark up the text, or jump in and create entries on the fly, go through the whole book and create a rough draft of the index.
- Step 4: Edit the index. Once the rough draft is written, go through again and edit all the entries and arrays. Editing may involve one pass or multiple passes.
- Step 5: Solicit feedback. Make sure that the index meets the needs of its readers by asking for feedback. Revise the index as needed.

• When the index is finished, it is ready to be typeset. This is usually handled by the book designer. Once typeset, review the proofs to make sure that the layout is correct.

• A list of key terms may be helpful to guide your decision making as you index. However, an index is much more than a searchable list of terms. The search tool can be used to assist your indexing process, but is not a substitute to reading the book yourself.

• Sometimes, changes are made to the text after the index is written, or a new edition of the book is released. If changes to the text are substantial, it is usually easier to write a new index from scratch. If changes are minimal, it may be possible to reuse and update the existing index.

TRY THIS

It is finally time to write your index:

- Have you blocked off time to write the index?
- How will you write the index? Are you going to use software or a manual method? Do you want to try marking up the text? What kind of editing approach would you like to try? You can, of course, also change your approach partway through.

- Writing an index is a big task. Think about how to break up the work into smaller chunks, such as a certain number of pages or chapters per work session.
- Take a moment to review the indexing specifications from the publisher or the formatting decisions you have made for yourself.
- Once the index is finished, who can you ask for feedback?
- Thinking further ahead, do you need to make time to design the layout, or to proofread the typeset index?

7

The Finer Points of Indexing

THIS BOOK HAS SO FAR discussed the different components of an index, how to select terms and create the structure and format, and the process for writing an index. At this point, you have what you need to start.

If you would like to go deeper, or if specific questions arise while you index, you may find answers in the following two chapters. This chapter covers some of the finer points of indexing, looking at ways to add polish and to navigate potentially tricky situations. The next chapter offers tips and suggestions for indexing a variety of topics and types of books and other material.

An important part of indexing is paying attention to the details. In these chapters, I try to show what that looks like.

CONSISTENCY

Consistency is key. Being consistent reinforces for readers that they understand how the index works. Being inconsistent breaks that promise.

Following the formatting conventions is an important part of maintaining consistency. Except for a possible headnote, indexes do not come with a user manual. Readers rely on indexes following certain conventions in order to be confident that they will know how to use the index that is now in front of them. As seen earlier in this book, conventions can vary somewhat, for example, letter-by-letter versus word-by-word alphabetical sorting, though they are usually not wildly different from each other. What is important is to choose one approach or another, and then stick to it.

Each book is also unique, and so some decisions may be specific for that index. For example, glosses may be used for names of royalty or to indicate family relationships, or a certain structure is used to indicate the relationship between the metatopic and the supermain discussions. As readers use the index, they are also, consciously or unconsciously, learning how this particular index functions. So it is also important to be internally consistent with the decisions made for this particular index. If glosses are used to clarify who the royalty are, then all royal names should have a similar gloss.

It may be difficult to remember all the different decisions that have been made and to consistently apply them throughout the index. Perhaps keep a list of decisions, or at least of different possibilities, as you write the rough draft. When editing the index, settle on a final decision, and edit with an eye toward consistency. It may also help to edit using multiple passes, with each pass focused on a different decision or element.

I realize that being consistent may seem boring, both when writing the index and in the final product. The purpose of an index is to guide and direct, and while writing an index is a creative process, an index also needs to be predictable and reliable. Being consistent is your friend for creating an index that readers will want to use.

COMPREHENSIVENESS

Indexes should also be comprehensive, that is, they should adequately cover all aspects of the text.

One way to think about comprehensiveness is to equate it with being detailed. That is partly true, and for myself, I like to write very detailed indexes. But not every index needs to be so granular, and there is a bit more to being comprehensive.

The index should be appropriate for the text. Audience is one consideration, as entries that are not relevant or necessary for the audience should be excluded. Space for the index should also be considered. If space is tight, there may not be room for everything, and so decisions will have to be made about where to focus the index and what to exclude.

Context is also important. *Recognition and Revelation*, edited by Nora Foster Stovel, gathers a diverse collection of essays by the twentieth-century Canadian author Margaret Laurence. One five-page essay is about typewriters. Within the essay, Laurence goes into detail about specific types and models of typewriters, including pet names for typewriters she has owned. Are these details indexable? I decided no, and simply created a single main heading for typewriters, which I also double-posted under a couple of other arrays. If Laurence had written an entire book about typewriters, then the discussion about specific models and personal favorites would be much more significant, and would be indexable. But in the context of fifty wide-ranging essays, I did not think that readers would search for such specific details. Typewriters, by itself, was comprehensive enough.

Specificity is another factor. Is it a typewriter or an Olympia Monica typewriter? A dog or a cocker spaniel? An apple or a Golden Delicious? Depending on the context and audience, it could be one or the other, or both. Being comprehensive does not always mean being the most specific, if that level of specificity is not necessary.

Think of a deep index versus a shallow index. A deep index includes entries for the full hierarchy of information, from the broad to the granular, so that readers have entry points at all levels. This would be a very detailed index, suitable for a scholarly or reference book. A shallow index is flatter, more focused on just one or two levels. The focus could be broad, on the metatopic and supermain and regular discussions, or it could be more granular, focused on the regular discussions and smaller details. This might be best if space is limited, or for a guide book, for example, which has a very specific focus and audience. In both cases, whether deep or shallow, if the index is appropriate to the text, then the index is appropriately comprehensive.

When thinking about whether the index should be deep or shallow, it is also important to remember that you have control over how comprehensive the index is. You decide how much or how little goes into the index and how headings and subheadings are phrased. Use your decision making as a tool. Pay attention to the text and the audience and craft an index that is just the right amount of comprehensiveness.

HEADNOTES AND EXPLANATORY NOTES

A headnote, or explanatory note, is a brief explanation about elements of the index that are not self-evident. If the index follows common indexing conventions, then a headnote is not necessary. If the index introduces an unfamiliar element or special formatting, then a headnote may be helpful to prevent confusion among readers.

I often use a headnote to explain how locators for figures, tables, and other illustrations are handled. A simple example might be as follows:

> *Illustrations are indicated by page numbers in italics.*

Other situations could be to explain how unfamiliar names are indexed, or how unusual elements, such as letters or journal entries, are handled. A good example of a lengthier headnote for a complex index is in *The Letterbooks of John Evelyn, volumes 1 and 2*, edited by Douglas D.C. Chambers and David Galbraith and indexed by Mary Newberry.

> *This index is necessarily selective. It can be used in conjunction with the electronic version of the text, published simultaneously by the University of Toronto Press, and with de Beer's great (in both bulk and merit) volume-length index to The Diary of John Evelyn, either in print, or in the version available through Oxford Scholarly Editions Online.*
>
> *Entries for Evelyn's correspondents list page numbers for their letters in bold. The page numbers are preceded by the letter number enclosed in parentheses. Page numbers in italics refer to figures and*

plates. References to "the Protestant lady's library" refer to the list Evelyn provided to Anne Spencer in Letter 543.

Biographical information is referenced under "about" and found at the beginning of an entry. Incidental mentions are indexed under "mentioned" and are found at the end of an entry.

If there is space, children's books can benefit from a lengthier headnote. Children are often learning how to use an index, and a short paragraph, using simple language, can provide instructions on how to use the index.

Headnotes are often placed at the beginning, or head, of the index. However, the latest NISO standards for indexing (ANSI/NISO Z39.4–2021) suggest placing the explanatory note as running headers or footers on each page, as readers can access the index at any point and may not see the note if placed at the beginning.

UNDIFFERENTIATED AND UNRULY LOCATORS

If locators do not appear approachable, then readers may be scared off from using the index.

This chiefly happens when there are long strings of undifferentiated locators. By undifferentiated, I mean a row of locators without subheadings. For arrays with just a few locators, this is not a problem. Most people would be comfortable looking up three or seven locators to find the information they want. But what about asking readers to look up ten locators? Fifteen? Twenty? Fifty? At a certain point, readers are going to give up.

This is why subheadings are so important. For large arrays, subheadings pre-sort the locators on behalf of the reader, so that the reader can easily narrow their search and not waste time or feel discouraged.

Consider this example from *Ancient Bones: Uncovering the Astonishing New Story of How We Became Human*, by Madelaine Böhme, Rüdiger Braun, and Florian Breier. Migration is a recurring topic throughout the book. Without subheadings, the array would have looked like this, with seventeen locators.

> migration, 45, 62–63, 66, 68, 139–141, 142–146, 181–182, 183–184, 192–194, 209–210, 219–221, 226–227, 266, 271, 290–291, 315n46, 319n15

With subheadings, the array looks like this:

> migration
>   between Africa and Eurasia, 62–63, 66, 68, 183, 192–94, 271, 291
>   assumptions about, 209–10
>   from climate change, 181–82, 183–84, 290–91
>   Darwin on, 45
>   factors for successful migration, 219–20
>   from Messinian Salinity Crisis, 192–94
>   Out of Africa theory, 139–41
>   Out of Africa theory, challenges to, 142–46, 226–27, 266
>   seafaring, 220–21, 315n46, 319n15
>   wanderlust, 227

The subheadings make the array much more approachable and meaningful. Instead of having to look up each locator themselves, readers can skim the list of subheadings and make a more informed choice.

The caveat is that subheadings should reflect meaningful distinctions. It does not help the reader to create subheadings simply for the sake of separating locators into smaller groups, if the groups themselves are arbitrary. In some situations, there is no meaningful way to break down a long string of locators. In other situations, there may not be enough space in the index for all the subheadings, or subheadings may not otherwise be practical.

I faced this situation when indexing *She Made Them Family: A Wartime Scrapbook from the Prairies*, by Anne Gafiuk. This is a book of local history, and quotes extensively from people who remember life during the Second World War. Often, these comments are just a sentence here and there. Including subheadings for all these mentions would have led to large arrays, which seemed unwieldy and out of proportion to how brief these comments often were. At the same time, I thought it important to pick up these mentions, especially if these people wanted to find themselves in the index, or for their family and friends who might search. My solution was to gather these mentions together as a long string of locators, but under the subheading "reminiscences of," which in some cases, if there were no other subheadings, I instead appended to the main heading. This way, readers are still given some idea for what these locators are about, while sidestepping a long and detailed array.

> Gavel, Len (Army)
>   in Army, 123–24, 335
>   life after Army, 124–25
>   reminiscences of, 48, 75, 78, 81, 82, 83, 91, 94, 100, 110, 111, 113, 115, 117, 121, 129, 130, 131, 132, 136, 137, 138, 139, 143, 145, 146
> Wedderburn, Lawrie, reminiscences of, 28, 43, 58, 60, 62, 63, 72, 82, 89, 111, 112, 113, 117, 119, 127, 128, 129, 130, 132, 136, 138, 139, 144, 270, 296

How many locators are too many? This can vary from array to array and book to book. In some cases, it may be important to distinguish between related concepts, such as chemical versus electrical propulsion in spacecraft, and so subheadings can be used even if there are only two or three locators. More often, the rule of thumb, for scholarly books, is to include subheadings if there are more than five to seven locators. For trade books, you could have up to eight or ten locators before you break them down into subheadings. This assumes that scholarly indexes should be more detailed, and that trade indexes can be less detailed. Different publishers and indexers can also have their preferred cut-off. As in the example above from *She Made Them Family*, I also tend to allow longer strings in subheadings, as the subheading clarifies what the locators are about.

Whatever you choose, try to be consistent. While space constraints may mean that some arrays have longer strings of locators than others, indexes look better and are easier to navigate if arrays are consistent in how locators and subheadings are handled.

In contrast to undifferentiated locators, unruly locators are when a mix of undifferentiated locators and subheadings are used in the same array. The unruly locators are the ones immediately following the main heading, without subheadings.

Returning to the migration example, say I wrote the array like this:

Migration, **45, 192–94, 209–10, 219–20, 227**
    between Africa and Eurasia, 62–63, 66, 68, 183, 192–94, 271, 291
    from climate change, 181–82, 183–84, 290–91
    Out of Africa theory, 139–41
    Out of Africa theory, challenges to, 142–46, 226–27, 266
    seafaring, 220–21, 315n46, 319n15

The question I always ask myself, when I see arrays like this, is what do those initial locators (in bold, for the sake of this example) signify? Are they unimportant, or less important than the subheadings? In which case, why include at all? Conversely, are they the most important locators? Then why not tell me using a subheading? In my experience, indexers often each have their own interpretation for what these unruly locators mean, and if indexers cannot agree, I suspect readers are left confused as well. I think it is much better to remove ambiguity by either having no subheadings or assigning all locators to a subheading.

That said, there are a couple of exceptions that I use, which I hope are clear to readers. One is if there are just a few locators, and one or more of them refer to an indexable creative or scholarly work. In these cases, I only provide a subheading for the work, as providing subheadings for each locator takes up space, which the index may not have, and seems disproportionate for just a few locators. The takeaway—I hope—for readers, is that the unruly locators are where the person is discussed, and the subheadings are where their works are discussed.

Haraway, Donna, 56, 77, 89–90
　"A Cyborg Manifesto," 56, 143
Michelangelo, 34
　David, 45–46, 66
　Sistine Chapel, 77–80

The second exception is to include a long range, for a large discussion, which is then broken down in the subheadings. This allows readers to either choose to read the whole discussion or to find what they want within the discussion. I used this in the index for *Accordion Revolution*, by Bruce Triggs. The section on garage band accordionists, for example, is a longer range, within which the author discusses specific accordionists and bands.

garage band accordionists, 360–68
　Angry, 364–65
　Bop-Kats, 361–62
　Chessmen, 365–66
　Joey Dee and the Starliters, 360
　Devil's Anvil, 367–68
　Galaxies IV, 366–67
　Gary Lewis and the Playboys, 362–64
　Three Chuckles, 360–61

In addition to undifferentiated and unruly locators, a third issue is when there are references on consecutive pages, but the discussion is not continuous. Going back to the example from *She Made Them Family*, this can be seen in a couple of places under the Len Gavel array: "81, 82, 83," "110, 111," "129, 130, 131, 132," "136, 137, 138, 139," and "145, 146." Should these locators be turned into ranges? Some indexers say yes, especially if space is tight. A range is more space efficient and will cut down on the number of locators. While I respect that approach, I prefer to keep the locators separate. The reason is because ranges, ideally, are for discussions that continue across pages. If the discussion is not continuous, and is instead separate discussions or mentions that just so happen to fall on consecutive pages, I think it is more honest and accurate to keep the locators separate.

Locators are key for directing readers to the text. When possible, ensure that locators are accessible and approachable, using relevant subheadings to split locators into smaller groups.

FOOTNOTES AND ENDNOTES

Footnotes and endnotes are indexable if they include substantive information that adds to the discussion. They are not indexable when they are citations. This is an important distinction, and goes back to the purpose of the index, which is to direct readers toward what the discussion is about. While citations are important, the index is not the right place for them.

How extensively the notes need to be indexed will vary from book to book. I often find that the endnotes in trade books are entirely citations and can be ignored. In scholarly books, some authors primarily use the notes for citations, while others make extensive use of the notes to provide additional information. Either way, it is worth scanning all the notes to see whether there is anything to pick up.

When picking up entries, it can sometimes be challenging to figure out what the note means, and it is necessary to refer to the main text to understand the full context. To make this easier, print or create a separate PDF of the endnotes to more easily match the notes to the text and determine what the appropriate entries should be.

Another issue to look out for is that the line between what is substantive and what is a citation can be slippery. You may have to make a judgment call that others could legitimately challenge. For example, consider the following endnotes from *The Bomb in the Wilderness*, by John O'Brian.

1. Susan Sontag's *On Photography* (New York: Doubleday, 1977) and her *Regarding the Pain of Others* (New York: Farrar, Straus and Giroux, 2003) address the relationship of photography to historical events.

2. In *The Nuclear Century: Voices of the Hibakusha of the World* (Tokyo: Japan Peace Museum, 1997), the story of the hibakusha is told in a combination of photographs and texts.
3. Some uranium for the bombs was also mined in the Belgian Congo and the United States.
4. In addition to his work in photography and film, Richard Finnie had a career as a writer and lecturer. Peter Geller, *Northern Exposures: Photographing and Filming the Canadian North, 1920–1945* (Vancouver: UBC Press, 2004), 135.
5. Robert Frank, quoted in Sarah Greenough and Philip Brookman, eds., *Robert Frank: Moving Out* (Washington, DC: National Gallery of Art, 1994), 54.
6. Sally Stein, "The Rhetoric of the Colorful and the Colorless: American Photography and Material Culture between the Wars" (PhD diss., Yale University, 1991).
7. Laura Pitkanen and Matthew Farish argue that the United States is heavily overrepresented in the arena of nuclear studies because of its long-standing nuclear weapons program and "the relative accessibility of research sites and data." Laura Pitkanen and Matthew Farish, "Nuclear Landscapes," *Progress in Human Geography* (August 31, 2017): 2, https://doi.org/10.1177/0309132517725808.

I did not index Susan Sontag or her books from the first note, as I decided that that was a citation. In hindsight, I think I made the wrong call. I did, however, index the second note, creating entries for hibakusha and *The Nuclear Century* (Japan Peace Museum). I still stand by that decision, though I also recognize that another indexer might choose differently.

I also created an entry for note 3, for uranium, as that is the subject of the note, but not for Belgian Congo or the United States. For note 4, I created an entry for Richard Finnie, but not for Peter Geller, which is a citation. I also did not create entries for notes 5 and 6, which are also citations.

For note 7, I created four entries. One each for Laura Pitkanen and Matthew Farish, as well as subheadings under "nuclear activities" and "United States of America."

All together, the entries that I created for these seven notes look like this:

Farish, Matthew, 164*n*7
Finnie, Richard, 164*n*4
hibakusha, 164*n*2
nuclear activities
    literature on, 164*n*7
The Nuclear Century (Japan Peace Museum), 164*n*2
Pitkanen, Laura, 164*n*7
United States of America
    nuclear studies and, 164*n*7
uranium
    sources of for nuclear bombs, 164*n*3

To indicate a note, the locator should include the page number that the note appears on, an *n* to indicate the note, and the note number. In the example above, the *n* is in italics, which is what that publisher prefers, but many publishers are fine without the italics or have their own preferred format. Check your publisher's guidelines to see if they have a preference.

If there are two or more notes in a row on the same topic, then use a double n and a range for the note numbers (342nn45–47). If a topic appears on the same page in non-consecutive notes, then the notes are indexed separately (342n45, 342n47, 342n52). If two notes with the same number appear on the same page, you can leave it to the reader to figure out which is which, or you can include the chapter within the locator (250n2 (chap. 3), 250n2 (chap. 4)).

WORDING

As I discuss in chapter 3, term selection should be based on what the text is about and what the audience expects and needs. Once terms are selected, what is the best way to phrase and present those terms? That is what I discuss in this section, as well as in the following sections on jargon, terms of art, plain language, neutral language, and offensive language.

When phrasing terms, the meaning should be absolutely clear. Terms should also be succinct and easy to scan, though clarity should take precedence, if the most succinct option is ambiguous. Adding a gloss may help provide clarity.

Main headings are usually written as nouns—people, places, organizations, concepts, things. Be concrete. While the meaning of the heading needs to match the text, the actual wording does not.

Subheadings can be more descriptive, while still focused on aboutness. When breaking down large discussions, link the subheading to the larger context (usually the main heading) so that a full picture of the discussion emerges.

If the main heading is a phrase, lead with the subject, as that is what readers are likely to search. Try to also lead with the subject in subheadings, especially in indented format. This makes the list of subheadings easier to scan. In run-in format, however, inverting phrases can make the array more difficult to read, and a more natural flow may be better. For example, here are some main headings for weather challenges, which are then gathered in larger arrays, in both indented and run-in formats.

    fog, pea soup
    heat, extreme
    rain, torrential
    snow, shoveling
    weather challenges
        fog, pea soup
        heat, extreme
        rain, torrential
        snow, shoveling

or

        weather challenges: extreme heat; pea soup fog; snow shoveling; torrential rain

JARGON, TERMS OF ART, AND PLAIN LANGUAGE

It is important to select terms that readers will understand. This involves taking into consideration audience knowledge and expectations and how well that matches the terms used in the text.

Many fields and disciplines use specialized terminology that outsiders may not necessarily know. This can be described as jargon, terms of art, or technical terms. Jargon can have a more negative connotation, implying that the language is intentionally difficult for outsiders to understand. Terms of art and technical terms are more positive, implying that it is necessary and useful to have a precise vocabulary, so that everyone involved knows exactly what is being discussed. Indexing, as seen throughout this book and in the glossary, has its own terms of art.

When relevant to the discussion, these technical terms should be used in the index, as part of accurately reflecting the text. The question, though, is whether readers will know these terms. If the book is being written for a specialized audience, then you can assume that readers will know the correct terms to search for. If the book is not written for a specialized audience, or if the audience is mixed, then the index needs to be made more accessible. Still use the technical terms, even as the preferred terms, and also include cross-references or double-posts under alternative terms. Try to think from the perspective of a student or a layperson in the field.

When using terms of art, I will also often ensure that the subheadings are written using plain language. I want the array, as a whole, to be accessible to as wide an audience as possible.

Another plain language consideration is translating descriptive language in the text into terms more suitable for the index. This is drilling down into the aboutness of the text. In some cases, chapter and section titles are evocative, which are intriguing and entertaining, but do not work well within an index. Or, a passage can be descriptive without explicitly stating what the discussion is about. As the indexer, you need to read between the lines and state in the index the aboutness of the passage.

I had to do this when indexing *Uncommon Sense: Shift Your Thinking, Take New Action, Boost Your Sales*, by Jill Harrington. This is a delightful and engaging business book about sales, but quite difficult to index as the author rarely outright stated what the discussions were about. For example, here are the chapter and section titles from chapter 2:

> Access: Get in Front of Good Prospects Faster
> > Your prospecting mind-set matters
> > Stop kissing frogs
> > Caution: Incoming frogs
> > Evidence is TOP of mind
> > Why your messages fail
> > Never say this!
> > Stop calling high
> > Make the shift

What does any of this mean? These titles suggest a few possible terms that might work in the index—access, prospects, mind-set, evidence, failure—but it is not entirely clear what to expect from this chapter. While other terms, especially frogs, are not suitable for the index, as frog is clearly being used as a metaphor.

To translate these titles into usable terms, I had to first read the chapter and find the key terms. In some cases, the key term was buried toward the end of the discussion. I also spent time researching sales terminology online to ensure I was using the right terms for this audience. With this new knowledge, I translated these chapter and section titles into the following, from which I was able to select terms for the index.

> prospecting
> > mind-set
> > VIP prospects
> > incoming leads
> > researching prospects
> > reasons for failure

statements to avoid
contacting executives
overview

These terms are not nearly as flashy as the original, but they are easily understood. There can be space in the index to match the tone of the book, including a cheeky, comic tone, but ultimately the index needs to be clear. Keeping the language plain and simple, while also using appropriate terms of art and keeping the audience in mind, will help ensure that readers understand the terms that they encounter.

NEUTRAL LANGUAGE

In addition to being clearly understood, the language used in the index should also be neutral and unbiased. The language should be honest about what is contained within the text, without trying to obfuscate or impose our own perspectives.

Being neutral can sometimes be a challenge, especially if the book is written by someone who has strong views, different from our own. If indexing your own book, and you stake out certain positions, it may also be a challenge to take a step back. But it is important to remember that the index is just a map to the text. The index is too condensed to fully lay out the arguments. Nor do you know the reader's position. You do not want to alienate the reader before they even get to the discussion. Let the index be neutral ground.

For main headings, using neutral language is often a matter of simply stating what the concept, person, or thing is, without further commentary. For example, a discussion about the pros and cons of speed limits can be expressed by the following heading:

speed limits

If subheadings are used, keep the subheadings factual and to the point. For example, the text may argue for or against specific policies in relation to highways and school zones, or different experts may have opposing views, but those views do not necessarily need to be reflected in the index.

> speed limits
>   for highways
>   Ibekwe on
>   Lee on
>   legislation on
>   pedestrians and
>   in residential neighborhoods
>   in school zones

Sometimes, though, it may be worth highlighting in the index that certain stances are being taken. Perhaps the discussions for and against are lengthy, and readers would appreciate quickly seeing where those arguments are. This can be done while keeping the language neutral and the discussion firmly in the text. In the example below, readers can begin to see the contours of the arguments, but still need to read the text for the full details.

> speed limits
>   for highways
>   Ibekwe for
>   Lee against
>   legislation mandating
>   pedestrians for
>   in residential neighborhoods
>   in school zones

Let's consider a much more challenging example, from a Holocaust memoir. Warning: this is difficult and emotional subject matter. It's okay if you'd rather skip the rest of this section.

It is important to emphasize that the emotion itself is not a problem. The Holocaust was horrific. Holocaust memoirs are often difficult to read. These stories should evoke emotional responses, and readers coming to the book are likely expecting to feel that emotion.

When indexing difficult subject matter like this, I think that being neutral means being honest, while also sticking to the facts. As the indexer, I want to avoid trying to whitewash or sugarcoat the events or introducing my own emotion or interpretation. While the facts are emotional, the best way I can serve the reader is to keep the entries simple and to the point, focused on what the text is about.

I tried to do this when indexing *Confronting Devastation: Memoirs of Holocaust Survivors from Hungary*, edited by Ferenc Laczó, as you can see in the following two arrays, for the Auschwitz-Birkenau concentration camps and Miriam Mózes. Also note that Mózes's array has three unruly locators not placed under subheadings. These ranges denote the three locations in the book where her memoir appears. The book was arranged chronologically and thematically, with several of the memoirs split up and placed accordingly.

>Auschwitz-Birkenau concentration camps
>   introduction, 132–33
>   death march from, 164–65, 349
>   deportation to, 138–41, 150–52, 162, 173–74
>   forced farm labour, 176–77
>   Jews saved from by Milakovics, 92
>   life at, 141, 152–54, 174–76, 177–78, 305–6
>   loss of family at, 105, 119
>   Neu-Dachs forced labour camp, 162–64
>   religious life at, 153–54
>   selection process, 152–53, 175
>Mózes, Miriam, 47–52, 183–87, 329–30
>   deportation to Austria, 52, 185–86
>   facing the thought of death, 186–87
>   German occupation and eviction from home, 183–84
>   liberation from Theresienstadt, 329
>   at Reformed (Calvinist) Gimnázium, 47–52
>   return home to Budapest and Hódmezővásárhely, 330
>   in Theresienstadt ghetto, 186

OFFENSIVE LANGUAGE

Sometimes, terms used in the text can be outright offensive. This can be particularly true for terminology about age, ability/disability, gender, sexuality, and race. These terms may be used, whether intentionally or unintentionally, in contemporary books, and can also be found in older books and historical documents, whether republished or quoted.

Indexers tend to fall into two groups on how to handle offensive terms. One perspective is that the index should take its cue from the text, full stop. As much as the indexer may disagree, it is not the indexer's role to decide which terms are used in the book, and consequently, which terms are used in the index. The opposing perspective is that language matters, and that indexers should be sensitive to how readers may perceive terms.

To start, try pointing out the offensive term to the author. The author may be unaware and may be willing to revise the book. If the author is not willing, or if the terms are from a historical document or a new edition of an older text in which the original wording is being maintained, then the index will need to address the offensive terms, one way or another.

Especially for historical documents, I think there is a case for including the offensive terms in the index. The index should reflect the text, and leaving out those terms may make it more difficult to access the relevant discussions. I also believe that historical documents should be preserved intact, albeit with appropriate context and acknowledgment that terminology has changed.

However, I think that there is also room to include additional terms in the index. Contemporary and inoffensive terms can be used as either the preferred term, with a cross-reference from the offensive term, or as a cross-reference to the preferred term within the index. This serves all readers, while also indicating to readers that alternative—and better—terms exist. This also helps to future-proof the index. While it is impossible to fully anticipate how language will change, including contemporary terms better serves readers who may not be aware of older terms.

NAMES

Names can be surprisingly tricky to index. Everyone has a name. We all live within cultures that have naming conventions. The trick is to realize that some of the names in the text may follow conventions that we are not familiar with.

Western names typically follow the structure of first name, middle name(s), and surname, in that order. When indexed, the name is inverted so that the surname comes first, with a comma between the surname and the rest of the name.

Other cultures and time periods can have different conventions. Medieval and premodern names often do not have a surname, and so the name is not inverted and should be sorted by first name. Spanish names can have compound first names and/or surnames, and it may be tricky identifying where to invert. Chinese, Japanese, and Korean names are traditionally written surname first and do not need to be inverted, unless the name is written in the text in the Western format (for example, for someone who is Korean American). When indexing, it is important to properly identify the different components of the name and to index accordingly, instead of assuming that all names follow the convention you are most familiar with.

Another potential issue is that names can change. Some people change their surnames upon marriage or adoption. In some monastic traditions, monks and nuns are given a new name upon taking their vows. Clergy may also be given or choose a new name upon ordination or elevation to a new role, a well-known example being the pope. Artists, performers, and writers may choose to use a stage name or pseudonym. Transgender and nonbinary people may choose a new name to better reflect their identity.

If only one name is used in the text, then that is most likely the preferred name to use in the index. If multiple names are used in the text, then decide which to make the main entry and include the other name(s) as a gloss and/or cross-reference. Consider both how the person self-identifies, as well as how the person is commonly and publicly known.

In some cases, the other name(s) will not be well-known and can be left out, and in other cases, they should be included as entry points.

Another consideration is whether to include titles and positions, such as king, countess, doctor, priest, actress. Include if these are important for identifying the person, especially if they are only referred to by a single name, either first name or surname. Also include if the audience may expect or appreciate it, for example, in a local history of a religious community in which readers have a personal connection to the people discussed. On the other hand, if the name is already complete, with a first name and surname, and the title or position is not needed for identification, then these can often be left out. Either way, be consistent in how titles and positions are handled.

When indexing names, be aware of the limits of your own knowledge. If there are names from a language, culture, or time period that you are not familiar with, take a moment to learn more about these names so that you can properly index them. For more information, the indexing chapter in the *Chicago Manual of Style* discusses a variety of names. The journal *The Indexer* has also published several articles on names. There is also an entire book, *Indexing Names*, edited by Noeline Bridge, that may be helpful. Librarians at university libraries can also be a good resource, as can some online research. Once, for a memoir set in Vietnam, I was able to find a page from a Vietnamese literature wiki that answered most of my questions.

GLOSSES

A gloss is a brief tag of additional information, usually enclosed in parentheses. It is a quick message to the reader to narrow the scope of a term or to provide confirmation that this is indeed what the reader expects. They are usually used with main headings, and can sometimes also be appropriate in subheadings. Glosses can be useful in many situations, though only use if needed for clarity.

One common use is for names, such as for royalty, nobility, clergy, or people identified in the text by only a partial name. This is particularly useful if a full name or surname is not available.

> Francis (pope)
> Margrethe II (Danish queen)
> Smith (cabinetmaker)
> William (Prince of Wales)

Glosses can also be used in biographies and memoirs to indicate relationships within a family, especially if the family is extensive and it is difficult to keep track of who is who. The relationship indicated can either be to the subject of the biography or to indicate the most significant relationship that that person has in the text. In the fictitious example below, Adeline Nickel is the subject, and so is the only one without a gloss.

> Nickel, Adeline
> Nickel, Fred (father)
> Nickel, Joseph (brother)
> Nickel, Kelly (Joseph's wife)
> Nickel, Rebecca (mother)
> Nickel, Zahara (aunt)
> Turner, Mary (Adeline's grandmother)

Glosses can also differentiate between two items or people sharing the same name.

> bats (animal)
> bats (baseball)
> Civil Rights Act (1866)
> Civil Rights Act (1964)
> Evans, Chris (actor)
> Evans, Chris (artist)

Another use for glosses is to enclose acronyms, if the acronym is used in the text. This provides an additional visual cue for readers who may be more familiar with the acronym than with the term spelled out. For certain well-known acronyms, such as NATO, it may be better to instead lead with the acronym and place the full name in parentheses.

> NATO (North Atlantic Treaty Organization)
> regional health authorities (RHAs)
> World Health Organization (WHO)

Glosses can also clarify geographical locations, especially for cities and towns that are not as widely known. In contrast, capitals and other well-known cities, such as New Delhi or San Francisco, probably do not need a gloss. For countries with states or provinces, either use postal code abbreviations or spell out the full name, depending on what you think the audience will understand.

> Aarhus (Denmark)
> Cairns (Queensland)
> Portland (ME)
> Portland (OR)

Glosses can also enclose dates for court cases and legislation.

> *Marbury v. Madison* (1803)
> Voting Rights Act (1965)

Glosses can also be used to indicate alternative terms when double-posting, so that readers can see both terms together and understand that they may find one or the other, or both, in the text.

> *Agalychnis callidryas* (red-eyed tree frog)
> Aisle (formerly Lunapads)
> autumn (fall)
> fall (autumn)
> Lunapads (now Aisle)

> red-eyed tree frog (*Agalychnis callidryas*)

Glosses can also be used for creative works, to either indicate the type of work or its author or creator. Depending on the context, it might also be appropriate to place multiple pieces of information in the parentheses.

> "Be Thou My Vision" (hymn)
> *Ink Shrimp* (Qi Baishi, 1947)
> *Jade City* (Lee)
> *Love & Revelation* (Over the Rhine, 2019 album)

A final use for glosses is to define terms from another language, ideally using the author's definition or translation. This can be useful in ethnographies or histories of other countries or cultures. These glosses should be brief, so as to not take up too much space, yet also long enough to be clear. In some cases, it may also be a good idea to double-post or include a cross-reference from the English translation.

I used glosses for translations in the index for *One or Two Words: Language and Politics in the Toraja Highlands of Indonesia*, by Aurora Donzelli. Language was a key element of the book, and it was important to index terms from the Toraja language. For example,

> *aluk* (rituals)
> *aluk rambu solo'* (rites of the smoke of the setting sun)
> *aluk rambu tuka'* (rites of the smoke of the rising sun)
> *aluk rampe matallo* (Rites of the East)
> *aluk rampe matampu'* (Rites of the West)
> *aluk to dolo* (ancestral religion)

So far this section has been about glosses in parentheses, which is my preferred method as I like the visual distinction that the parentheses provide. However, another option is to append the same information using a comma. I do not think that this works as well for all situations, such as family relationships, acronyms, and translations, but it does work for some situations, such as places, dates, and names. For example,

> Aarhus, Denmark
> Civil Rights Act, 1964
> William, Prince of Wales

Appending information using a comma can also be used to collapse subheadings. This is useful if there is only one subheading and, instead of deleting the subheading, it seems more helpful to include that same information at the main heading level. For example,

> mining
>   copper

can be rewritten as,

> mining, copper

or

> mining, for copper

ART, BOOKS, FILMS, MUSIC, NEWSPAPERS, AND OTHER CREATIVE WORKS

Creative works are often indexable, either as regular discussions or even supermain discussions, or as smaller details that are used as sources or illustrations.

When formatting the titles of creative works, art pieces, books, plays, movies, newspapers, magazines and journals, classical music, and music albums, should all be in italics. Titles of shorter works, such as short stories, poems, articles, and songs, should be in quotation marks.

As I discussed in the previous section, a gloss is often appropriate for identifying the author or creator. For works like newspapers and journals, or movies, TV shows, and podcasts, for which there may not be a single, identified creator, a generic gloss, identifying the type of work, may be appropriate instead.

When sorting titles of works, ignore articles (such as A, An, and The) but do sort prepositions (such as Of or On). Instead of simply ignoring articles, dropping the article or inverting the title are also options.

For example,

> "Cheek to Cheek" (song)
> "A Good Man is Hard to Find" (O'Connor)
> *Indexer* (journal)
> *Of Mice and Men* (Steinback)
> *Old Guitarist, The* (Picasso)

The same formatting and sorting conventions apply when indexing the work as a subheading. If the work is a subheading under the creator, then the gloss with the creator's name can be removed.

> Debussy, Claude
>   *Nocturnes*
> Hugo Award for Best Novel
>   *Ancillary Justice* (Leckie, 2014)
>   *The Calculating Stars* (Kowal, 2019)
>   *A Desolation Called Peace* (Martine, 2020)
>   *The Fifth Season* (Jemisin, 2016)
>   *A Memory Called Empire* (Martine, 2022)
>   *Network Effect* (Wells, 2021)
> NPR (National Public Radio)
>   *All Songs Considered* podcast

When indexing creative works, is it better to create standalone arrays, index as a subheading under the creator, or double-post?

Works that have a substantial discussion, especially if the array requires subheadings, should have their own standalone array. These are usually regular or supermain discussions, and should be treated as such.

For works that have more minor discussions or mentions, it depends on the context. To start, I like to index these as subheadings under the creator, so that all the creative works are gathered in one place. If there are just a few such works, or if the emphasis seems to be more on the work than the creator, or if I think that the audience will want to look up specific works, or if there is space in the index, I will also double-post these works as standalone arrays.

If there is a long list of works discussed, such as over ten or twenty, or even a hundred, I tend to only gather in one array under the creator and not double-post. At that volume, double-posting can add an extra page or two to the index, which there may not be space for, as well as potentially make the index feel cluttered. If different types of works by the same creator are discussed, I may use the em-dash-modified format to subdivide into separate arrays.

If there are separate arrays for both the creative work and the creator, be sure to link through cross-references so that readers can find both. I did this for *After Authority: Global Art Cinema and Political Transition*, by Kalling Heck. The book focuses on four films by four filmmakers from different countries, time periods, and political contexts. In each case, the primary film discussed was a supermain discussion and needed its own array. However, there were also brief discussions about each filmmaker and their other films. For filmmaker Roberto Rossellini, the arrays I created for him looked like this:

Germany Year Zero (Rossellini, 1948)
    introduction, 3, 4, 20, 24–25
    ambiguity as unwillingness to take stance, 25, 28–29, 40–42, 41, 44–45, 139
    ambiguity of national identity, 27
    cinematic context of, 25–26
    comparison to *Sátántangó* (Tarr, 1994), 50, 59, 69, 70
    comparison to *Woman on the Beach* (Hong, 2006), 84, 85, 104, 108
    distinction between authoritarianism and totalitarianism, 32
    Edmund's suicide, 29, 29–30, 44
    as empty signifier, 147–149
    failure of authority and, 32–34

    and free and rightless (vogelfrei), 42–44
    messianic hope in, 38, 39–40
    and openness and neoliberal logic, 45–49
    political critique by, 26–27
    ruins as repudiation of authoritarianism and glimpse to future, 34, 35–40, 37
    title of, 36, 38, 40
Paisa (Rossellini, 1946), 26, 27, 28
Rome, Open City (Rossellini, 1945), 26, 27, 28
Rossellini, Roberto, 27–28
    Paisa (1946), 26, 27, 28
    Rome, Open City (1945), 26, 27, 28
    See also *Germany Year Zero* (Rossellini, 1948)

The largest array is for the film *Germany Year Zero*, which represents the focus of discussion. But, I have also double-posted the two other films by Rossellini that are also mentioned. Rossellini's array also includes an unruly locator for biographical information, which is not ideal, but does save space. Given the focus of the book, I decided to prioritize the films. Rossellini's array also includes a cross-reference to *Germany Year Zero*, providing access for readers who start their search with the filmmaker.

Notice also that I include dates in the glosses, alongside the filmmakers. This was perhaps not strictly necessary, but given that the films were from different time periods, I thought that the dates might be helpful to orient readers to the different films. When indexing creative works, think about what would help the audience, as well as what will make the entry clear. It is not important to include every piece of information, but just enough for the reader to understand.

TRIAGE FOR SPACE CONSTRAINTS

In an ideal world, there is as much space as is needed for the index. The index can be as detailed as it needs to be, showcasing all the levels in the hierarchy of information and providing multiple access points.

It can be tricky, though, to pinpoint how long an ideal index should be, as every book is a little different. Nancy Mulvany, in *Indexing Books*, suggests that for trade books, the number of pages taken up by the index should equal 2–5 percent of the number of indexable pages. For two hundred indexable pages, this means that the index should occupy between four and ten pages. For texts with greater detail, such as scholarly books, textbooks, reference books, medical books, and cookbooks, Mulvany suggests that the index should be 7–8 percent of the text, or fourteen to sixteen pages of index for two hundred indexable pages. For texts such as documentation, manuals, and policies and procedures, Mulvany suggests 10 percent or more, or at least twenty pages. Keep in mind that the format of the index can also play a factor, with run-in format being more space efficient than indented format. In my experience, I often find Mulvany's estimates to be accurate. However, it is important to focus on writing an index appropriate to the text. Estimates like Mulvany's are a useful gauge, not a rule.

That said, it is not always possible to write a dream index. The challenge is that publishers may impose a limit on how long the index can be. That limit often has no relationship to the estimates provided by Mulvany, and so what ideally would be a sixteen-page index now needs to fit within twelve pages, for example.

The space constraint is often because books are printed on large sheets of paper called signatures. Each signature is folded and cut to create a series of pages, with multiple signatures bound together to form the book. Signatures can vary in length, and are always in multiples of four. From the publisher's perspective, increasing the length of the book is not a matter of just adding a page or two, but is a matter of adding four, eight, twelve, or sixteen pages, all of which are an additional cost. Instead of having to pay for several blank pages at the end of the book, because there is not enough material to fill an additional signature, the publisher may instead look for ways to save space, including a shorter index.

Being confronted with a space limit can be a real challenge. Writing a shorter index is not easier or faster. Having to write an index that is deliberately shorter than it would otherwise be requires making difficult decisions about what to simplify and leave out, because the reality is that not everything will fit.

Having to fit the index within a tight space is especially difficult if that limit comes as a surprise, after the index has already been written. The temptation—I've been there—is to panic and to slash entries, without much of a plan. Often, at this point, there is also the time pressure of meeting a deadline, which adds to the stress.

The index will be better, though, if you can plan before you start the index. If planning ahead is not possible, then at least to think through the cuts before they are made. The index will not be ideal, but at least it will be the best it can be under the circumstances.

I like to call this triaging. Triage comes from medicine and is a way to quickly determine how to allocate limited resources so that the most injured or sick, who still have a chance to survive, receive treatment first. Indexing is not a matter of life and death, but decisions can still be made about what is most important to prioritize and what can be let go.

If you know ahead of time that space will be limited, triage proactively, to guide decision making during the indexing process. If the index is still too long, or if you only learn after the index is written that it needs to be shortened, triage to evaluate the index and make informed decisions about how to trim.

To triage your index, follow these steps and considerations:

- Before starting the index, confirm with the publisher how much space is available. Ideally, the publisher can tell you how many lines will fit, along with how many characters per line. You can then adjust the margins to mimic the space available and count the number of lines in your index. Or, the publisher may tell you the number of pages reserved for the index, from which you will have to estimate as best you can. Try looking at other indexes from that publisher to gauge how the index will fit. The publisher may also have their own method for estimating length, which you should then use. If space looks like it will be tight, it can be worth expressing your concern and asking for more space. Additional space is not guaranteed, but I have sometimes been able to get a bit more.

- If the index is already written and is too long, determine by how much the index needs to be cut. Is it a few lines? Several lines? A page? Two pages? More? Knowing this will tell you whether superficial trims will be enough or whether the cuts need to be deeper. If you have already submitted the index, the designer may be able to try typesetting the index and tell you by how many lines it is over.

- Prioritize what must remain. This may sound counterintuitive, to first determine what to keep, but the index should remain an accurate reflection of the text. What are the main discussions that need to stay? Everything else, potentially, can go.

- Raise the bar for passing mentions. Passing mentions are snippets of information that are mentioned but not really discussed. Where to draw the line is somewhat subjective. If space is tight, the bar may need to be raised, and minor discussions and entries removed from the index. For example, perhaps there are people mentioned who would be nice to include, but who are also less likely to be searched.

- Remove subheadings. While I value subheadings, they can also take up a lot of space. Sometimes it is better to tolerate undifferentiated locators in order to squeeze the index into a tight space. One approach to removing subheadings is to raise the bar for when they are added. Instead of adding subheadings if there are more than six locators, perhaps only add if there are more than ten locators. Another approach is to reserve subheadings for the core metatopic and supermain arrays, while removing subheadings from arrays which are less important.

- Remove additional access points. While multiple access points improve usability, one access point is better than none. Fewer access points also mean that more different pieces of information can be crammed into the index.

- Be consistent. However you choose to cut, whether it is raising the bar for passing mentions, removing subheadings or access points, or all the above, try to do so consistently. Being consistent gives the impression that the index is still deliberately constructed, and is still a reliable finding aid.

Trimming the index beyond what feels right is never fun. It can feel like dismantling your prized creation, undoing hours of work. But it is sometimes necessary. Done well, shortening the index can also be done quickly while still preserving the heart and integrity of the index.

TAKEAWAYS

- Indexing is all about paying attention to the details.

- Strive to be consistent, with the format, structure, and how terms are phrased.

- Indexes should be comprehensive, though comprehensiveness is not simply being detailed. The amount of detail and specificity should be appropriate to the text and audience.

- Include a headnote or explanatory note to explain unusual or unique elements of the index.

- As a general rule, unruly locators and long strings of undifferentiated locators should be avoided, as their significance is not clear. Use subheadings instead.

- Substantive information in footnotes and endnotes are indexable. Citations are not.

- When selecting and phrasing terms, make sure that terms are clearly written, and that the most significant element of the term comes first. Use plain language, while also respecting and including jargon and terms of art that is appropriate for the audience.
- Avoid inserting your own bias into the index. Main headings and subheadings should be neutral and factual.
- Language changes, including our understanding of what is offensive. While the index should reflect the text, it is also possible to use contemporary and inclusive language within the index.
- Names are not always straightforward to index, especially names from an unfamiliar language or culture. If in doubt, consult resources to identify the different components of a name, to know how best to include in the index.
- For unclear terms, glosses can be appended to main headings to clarify what the term is about.
- Creative works, such as art, books, film, music, and media, have specific formatting requirements.
- If the index needs to be shortened to fit a tight space, create a plan by triaging. The resulting index may not be ideal, but it can still preserve the most important elements.

TRY THIS

Consider indexes written by others:

- Can you find any indexes that you could describe as exceptionally well written? What makes them stand out?
- Find some books similar to the one you are indexing. How well are those books indexed? What might you want to replicate or avoid?

Think now about your own index:

- Is there anything from this chapter that you would like to revisit in your index?
- Double-check with the publisher—how much space is available for the index? Does that space seem sufficient? Do you need to adjust your indexing approach for the index to fit?

8

Tips for Indexing Different Types of Books

THE PUBLISHING WORLD IS VAST, composed of all kinds of genres, subject matter, and audiences. The basics of indexing are applicable across the industry, and each niche can also have its own particularities, based on how the material is written and what the audience needs and expects.

My own experience is limited to certain sectors of publishing. I primarily index trade and scholarly books in the humanities and social sciences. I especially enjoy indexing history, religion, biography and memoir, and Asian studies. I also have experience in other areas, such as anthropology, sociology, political science, Indigenous studies, business books, and health books. I have also learned that there are subjects that I should avoid, such as philosophy. While I have the skills to probably piece together a decent index, not having the subject matter expertise can make these projects difficult and stressful. It is easier and more enjoyable to stick within my comfort zone. Most indexers, who index professionally, have their areas of expertise.

In this chapter, I offer tips for indexing various types of books. This is largely based on my own experience, which means that there are some areas I am not able to comment on. For those, I instead offer other resources that may prove helpful.

TRADE VERSUS SCHOLARLY

In publishing, books are commonly divided into two camps: trade and scholarly.

Trade books are written for a mass-market audience. Trade includes a wide range of subjects and audiences, including cookbooks, gardening books, guidebooks, how-to guides, self-help books, health books, business books, biographies and memoirs, popular history, and popular science. Most books at your local bookstore can be considered trade.

Scholarly, or academic, books, are written for a much narrower audience and are usually based on the author's academic research. These can range from books written for undergraduate students to books written for other scholars within a particular field. Mass-market appeal is not expected, though occasionally books can cross over into the trade market and become unexpected bestsellers. Scholarly books also tend to be published by university or scholarly presses, which is a separate part of the industry than the current Big Five publishers and other small press trade publishers.

Simply knowing whether your book is trade or scholarly can start to give you a sense for how to index.

Indexes for trade books can often be lighter. For some books, light means focusing more on the big picture, with arrays for the metatopic, supermain, and regular discussions. The bar for passing mentions can be raised, and slightly longer strings of locators can be tolerated. There may also be less space reserved for the index, which will require the index to be shorter. A light approach can also mean selecting the right details for the audience, as opposed to all the details. For example, a hiking guide should focus on trails, where trails are located (for example, national parks), and possibly scenic areas of interest, while mentions of wildlife and flowers glimpsed along the way can be left out.

Scholarly indexes, on the other hand, tend to have much more detailed indexes. This reflects the fact that scholarly books tend to be more dense, with tightly argued discussions, sources, and examples. Scholarly books are often used for research, and the index can be the primary access point, rather than the book being read cover to cover. The index needs to be thorough enough for readers to quickly see whether what they are looking for is discussed. Plan to create a more complex index structure, as well as to include more minor details and subheadings.

MONOGRAPHS VERSUS EDITED COLLECTIONS

Among books, there is also the distinction between monographs and edited collections. Monographs are books by a single author or co-authors, the book written as a unified whole. Edited collections gather a disparate set of chapters. These chapters are usually written by different authors, though can sometimes be a collection of essays by a single author. While the chapters usually center around a theme, each chapter is written independently of the others, and can cover a diverse range of topics. Edited collections are usually found in scholarly publishing, although sometimes also in trade.

Monographs can be straightforward to index. The book will have a metatopic, supermain discussions, regular discussions, and smaller details, from which terms can be selected and the index structured. Edited collections can be tricker to index.

The main complication is that the connection between chapters is much weaker. The overall subject of the book can serve as a metatopic, and the volume editors may draw out common themes in the introduction and/or conclusion. Otherwise, each chapter is autonomous. For example, a few years ago I indexed *Encounters Old and New in World History: Essays Inspired by Jerry H. Bentley*, edited by Alan Karras and Laura J. Mitchell. As seen in the title, world history was a theme that appeared in several chapters, along with Jerry H. Bentley. However, there were also chapters on topics as diverse as tuna fisheries in Spain, iguanas in the Caribbean, and *makgeolli*, a Korean alcoholic beverage.

I find it helpful to conceptualize indexing edited collections as writing a series of mini-indexes, one for each chapter, that are then mashed together. Each chapter will likely have its own metatopic array.

Supermain and regular discussions and arrays will be shorter, as these are mostly confined to individual chapters, resulting in fewer subheadings.

There should still be a metatopic array for the overarching subject of the book. Also look for themes that may span chapters. Chapters may also comment on the same subject from different perspectives. Thinking about the index as a mash-up of mini-indexes can make it easier to focus on what each chapter is doing, while also looking for how the chapters—and entries—intersect.

Another challenge with edited collections is that terminology can vary across chapters. That is, authors of different chapters may use different words to mean the same thing. The trick is to determine whether these chapters are all talking about the same thing (and so a single array can be created in the index, with cross-references from the other, similar terms), or whether the distinctions are meaningful enough to create separate arrays for all the terms.

A separate challenge is that each chapter can have its own theoretical approach and writing style, resulting in some chapters being easier or more difficult to index than others. I have indexed scholarly collections for which I submitted the index still not entirely sure what the author of one chapter was trying to say, while in other collections an author decided to use a creative methodology and present their research and findings in the form of a poem, which poses a different kind of challenge.

Otherwise, the indexes for edited collections should be much the same as for monographs. The indexes should accurately reflect the discussions and relationships within the book, and should be appropriate for the audience.

HISTORY

History is one of my favorite subjects to index. History is often about telling a story, and I much prefer stories to abstract arguments.

However, its narrative structure can also make history difficult to index. It can be a challenge to parse the different elements of the narrative, whether these are events happening within chronological time, or themes and topics, around which the narrative coalesces. Think about the big picture. What is the book about? How does the book break down the discussion? How can all of this translate into the metatopic, supermain, and regular discussions? These will be the building blocks for the index's structure.

History books are also often jammed with detail. Expect a lot of names, places, events, and organizations. Military histories will often include details about military units, for example, while an environmental history of an area will include details about local geographical features. This level of detail should be indexed, but it can lead to a longer index and can take more time.

When indexing, it may help to create the rough draft in two passes. The first pass can focus on the broad scope of the book, making sure that the metatopic, supermain, and regular discussions are all mapped in the index. The second pass can focus on picking up the smaller details. Dividing the work this way may help you to better focus and make sure that both aspects are represented in the index, while avoiding feeling overwhelmed by the volume of information. If there is a space limitation, focusing on the larger discussions first will also ensure that those make it in, with the smaller details fitting into whatever space is leftover, though to fit the space some details may have to be cut.

BIOGRAPHY, MEMOIR, AND FAMILY HISTORY

Similar to history, biographies, memoirs, and family histories also tell stories. Like history, there is often a lot of detail to pick up, and the narrative structure can also be a challenge to break down into smaller chunks for the index.

The challenge of biography and memoir is that the metatopic is so tightly bound to one person. How does one slice up a life? Chronologically? Thematically? The book's structure should provide some guidance for which are the supermain and regular discussions. Once identified, how should these translate into index arrays? Personally, I like to use the em-dash-modified format, which keeps all the entries together while also allowing meaningful distinctions between arrays. The alternative is to have arrays scattered throughout an index.

I discuss the em-dash-modified format on page 72, including for biography and memoir. I want to give one more example here, for *I Can Only Paint: The Story of Battlefield Artist Mary Riter Hamilton*, by Irene Gammel, that is both a biography and an art book. This biography is about the Canadian World War I battlefield artist Mary Riter Hamilton and is beautifully illustrated throughout with Hamilton's art. After reading the book, and in consultation with the author, we settled on the following entries (along with the first three subheadings for each):

> Hamilton, Mary Riter: about, 5-8, 10, 307; accolades received by, 266-8, 287, 299; antimodernism and, 32-5; ...
> Hamilton, Mary Riter, artwork: *Abazia* [sic] *di St Gregorio* (n.d., oil), 31; *Albert (Somme) Route d'Amiens* (1920, oil), 201-3, *202*; *Among the Ruins, Arras* (1919, oil), 146, 350n33; ...
> Hamilton, Mary Riter, exhibitions: Canadian War Museum (2018-19), 305; Fort Garry Hotel (1926), 292, 294-5; Galeries Simonson (Paris, 1922), 270; ...
> Hamilton, Mary Riter, locations visited and painted: Ablain-Saint-Nazaire, 96-7, 98, *99*, 101-3, 105-10, 113, 114, *117*, 119, 120, 124, 126; Albert, *xiv*, 201; Arras, *xiv*, 36, 75, 155, 156, 158, 160-1, 162, 164, 166-7; ...
> Hamilton, Mary Riter, war artist period: absence themes, 42, 85, 109-10, 188, 208; ambivalent role of, 343n51; androgynous ideal, 237; ...

Note, first of all, that instead of using em dashes, I simply reproduced Mary Riter Hamilton's name, with the same effect. Each of these is an array with subheadings. Since Hamilton's name is reproduced, the arrays are still held together, keeping everything about Hamilton in one place in the index.

Since this book was mostly focused on Hamilton's time as a battlefield artist, that is also the focus of these arrays. Instead of creating separate arrays for typical elements of a life—childhood, education, career, family life, relationships—which are common in many biographies and memoirs, those are gathered as subheadings under the first array, a general catchall for Hamilton's life. In contrast, discussions specific to her life and work as a battlefield artist are gathered in the last array.

The "artwork" array is long, containing entries for over a hundred paintings and drawings. To further differentiate the art, especially for works with similar titles, each array contains a gloss with the date and medium, if known. For example, *"Among the Ruins, Arras* (1919, oil)." I considered creating separate arrays for different mediums, such as oil, watercolor, and pastel, but that quickly became a challenge as a few works of art were difficult to categorize. In the end, the simplest option was to keep all the art together and to let the glosses differentiate. Keeping the entries broad and few in number can serve the reader better than creating a long list of narrowly focused arrays.

The "exhibitions" array gathers all of Hamilton's exhibitions, and the "locations visited and painted" array tracks Hamilton's movement across the war-torn landscape.

One aspect I needed to decide was which subheadings to double-post. For the art, I decided to not double-post. Due to the sheer volume of works, I was concerned that the index might feel bloated if these were double-posted. I also thought that the art would be easier to find if the works were all together. I did, however, double-post exhibitions and the locations where Hamilton worked. There were fewer entries for these arrays, and I thought it more likely that readers would want to search for specific places. It is okay to make different decisions for different arrays and types of information, so long as the information is clearly accessible one way or another.

Family histories are similar to biographies and memoirs in that they focus on people, but these books have a wider focus, covering multiple generations and places. The em-dash-modified format is probably not necessary, as the focus is not on a single person. The greater challenge is differentiating the family members.

Glosses can be useful for spelling out relationships, especially for people who share the same name. Glosses can also be used to identify who is married to whom and intergenerational relationships (grandparents, parents, children). If there are just a few names, then glosses may not be necessary. If a lot of names, readers may appreciate the help.

It is also important to pick up all family members, even minor mentions. You never know who contemporary family members are going to look up.

I also like to include an array for the family as a whole, as there is often some discussion that provides an overview. I force-sort this to the top of the list of family members, so that readers can learn about the family first before seeing the entries for the individual members. For example, for the Blondin family, in *Strangers in the House*, by Candace Savage, I created this array:

> Blondin (Sureau dit Blondin) family
>   ancestry, 27, 32–33, 35
>   attempt to link to Qu'Appelle Blondins, 35–36
>   author's search for Goose Lake Country homesteads, 125–27
>   departures from Goose Lake Country, 169, 173, 187–88
>   migrations by, 37–38
>   move to Goose Lake Country (SK), 94–95, 96, 97–98, 107, 109, 113–14, 116
>   move to Tiny Township (ON), 69–70
>   as outsiders, 148–49
>   surname origins, 26
>   *See also specific family members*

In addition to the family, think about what other information is important. What has shaped this family? Include entries for the places where this family has lived and worked. Pick up details about historical events that the family has lived through or participated in. People and families exist within a context, and that context is equally important to index.

LETTERS AND JOURNALS

A related genre to biography and memoir is the publication of letters and journals. These are often by a single person, providing details about their life and times through their perspective. In some cases, the letters may be the correspondence between two or more people.

The challenge is that letters and journals are often not written for public consumption. Thoughts may not be fully fleshed out. People and events may be alluded to. As the indexer, this can require reading between the lines to figure out the underlying aboutness.

Letters and journals can also lack a clear structure. There is still a metatopic, usually the author of the letters or journals, or perhaps the letters and journals have been edited to emphasize a certain theme. But letters and journals are typically not written according to an overarching plan, with supermain and regular discussions clearly spelled out. As the indexer, you will need to sort through all the details and figure out the significant topics and themes.

In journals and letters, all the details are fair game for indexing. Think about the letters and journals as both inward and outward facing. Inward, in that they are about and reflect the life of the writer, and outward, in that the writer is often commenting about events happening outside of them, whether their next-door neighbor, colleagues, or world-shattering events. The index should reflect both aspects. Think also about the intended audience for the book, whether that is a scholarly audience, fans, or family and friends. Also consider what was important to the author. For example, in *Margaret Laurence and Jack McClelland, Letters*, edited by Laura K. Davis and Linda M. Morra, which collects the letters between Canadian author Margaret Laurence and her publisher, the writing and publication of her books was a common and important topic, as well as their comments on the Canadian literary scene.

Letters and journals can be heavily annotated, with footnotes or endnotes providing context. There may also be a lengthy introduction, introducing the person and drawing out themes. These should all be indexed as well, and can also provide insight for what to include in the index or how to interpret obscure passages.

The index for these types of books may also be the primary access point to the text, especially if the intended audience is researchers. The index should include a lot of detail, even minor references that in other contexts may be considered passing mentions. When writing subheadings, it can be hard to categorize these, and a subheading like "mentioned" may be the simplest option to indicate their existence. While paying attention to detail, remember to also pay attention to the larger themes and topics which emerge, and around which the index can be structured.

Indexing letters and journals can be challenging because the form is amorphous and there can be so much detail to assess. Try to find some examples from other books. See which indexes are done well and which are done poorly. Both extremes should give you some ideas for what to either replicate or avoid.

HOW-TO AND SELF-HELP

How-to and self-help books are somewhat different from each other. How-to books seek to teach and explain. They are practical, and oriented outwards, to help the reader accomplish a concrete goal. Self-help books, in contrast, tend to be more inspirational and inward-focused.

How-to books tend to focus on facts and processes. The indexes should as well. Terms in the index should be simple and to the point. The index should also be thorough, for readers treating the book as a reference, instead of reading the book cover to cover.

The following example is from *How to Wash a Chicken: Mastering the Business Presentation*, by Tim Calkins. It is a very practical book, going step by step through creating and delivering a business presentation. The array below is from the chapter on delivery, which I turned into a super-main array. The array begins with a page range for the chapter, which is then broken down into subheadings. Most of the subheadings are concrete—clothes, confidence, eye contact, nerves, standing up. These are all things that presenters should consider, and as such, they are all double-posted as standalone arrays.

    delivery, 159–77
        introduction, 159
        closings, 177
        clothes, 164–65
        confidence, 162–63
        control of room, 212–13
        data use, 171–73, 207–8
        dealing with disagreements, 29, 175
        energy level, 163–64
        eye contact, 169–70
        ideal place to stand, 166–68
        key tips, 234–35
        nerves, 160–64
        presentation content and, 104
        reading the audience, 173–75
        slides, 169
        software tools, 211–12
        standing up, 165–66, 213
        starting point, 164, 168–69, 231
        by Steve Jobs, 201, 204–9
        as storytelling, 169
        time monitoring, 175–76
        transitions between presenters, 176–77
        trust in presentation, 170–71
        withholding information, 206–7

In contrast to how-to books, self-help books can be more difficult to index because the underlying aboutness is not always clear. The language used can be inspirational and emotive, which, while appropriate for the audience, can be difficult to translate into indexable terms. It can also be difficult to identify where discussions begin and end. There are often illustrative examples and people quoted, which are easy to pick up, but the underlying concepts may not be as clearly spelled out.

Try mind mapping or writing a summary to pin down the book's message and structure. Also pay attention to introductions and conclusions, which may outline where the book is going. Indexes for self-help books are often a bit shorter than other trade books because there is less concrete detail to pick up, but still make sure that the index provides access to significant discussions.

BUSINESS BOOKS

Business books can vary in how they are written. They are often structured around addressing or solving a specific issue, such as leadership, sales, or conflict management. As such, they can be similar to how-to books. Case studies and examples are common, either showcasing the author's experience or from elsewhere in the industry. The book may also contain proprietary concepts or frameworks, which the book is teaching. All of this should be indexed.

Some business books also contain an inspirational side, such as trying to encourage a mind-set or paradigm change within the reader. Like in self-help books, these concepts may be a little slippier to grasp. Whereas self-help books can be primarily focused on emotions, I find inspirational business books to still be grounded in whatever the larger issue is, which can make it easier to index.

GUIDEBOOKS

Guidebooks can be straightforward to index. The main challenge is deciding which details to pick up and which to exclude.

By guidebooks, I mean books like bird-watching guides, hiking guides, and travel guides. These are written for an audience with a specific reason for using that book. The index should cater to that reason. Otherwise, the index can become too long with extraneous details, which means that readers will need to spend more time searching for what they desire. There may also not be enough space in the book for a long index.

Let's look at an example from the index for *Destination Hikes: In and Around Southwestern British Columbia*, by Stephen Hui. The book discusses one hike per chapter, each chapter three to five pages long. I decided that the index should include the featured hikes, mountains (since most hikes take place on mountains or highlight mountains as scenic features), provincial and regional parks (since some of these hikes are in parks, and readers may want to search for parks that are nearby), local conservationists and authors (again, for local readers), and any particularly interesting and unusual features that the author highlights, such as giant trees.

I decided to exclude smaller trails and other details about specific hikes. For example, the Kennedy Falls hike follows or crosses paths with the Cedar Tree Trail, Kirkford mountain-bike path, and Kennedy Creek. While these are important details for navigation once onsite, I do not think that these are details that the reader will look up in the index. Simply indexing the feature hike—Kennedy Falls—is sufficient for directing readers to all that they need to know. The exception would be famous, destination trails, such as the Trans Canada Trail. Similarly, I also excluded entries about wildlife and plants, except for important safety information.

For the chapter on Kennedy Falls, this resulted in the following entries. Note that the chapter range for Kennedy Falls is in bold, to better highlight for readers the featured hikes. I also double-posted Kennedy Falls, along with Lynn Canyon Ecology Centre, under the North Shore, the geographical region these fall within, for readers interested in seeing hiking and activity options in the North Shore.

Kennedy Falls, **46–49**
Lynn Canyon Ecology Centre, 49
Lynn Creek Cedar, 48
Lynn Headwaters Regional Park, 47, 49
Lynn Peaks, 48
Mount Fromme, 46

The Needles, 48
North Shore
    Kennedy Falls, **46–49**
    Lynn Canyon Ecology Centre, 49
Stoltmann, Randy, 48
trees, giant, 48

Indexes for guidebooks can often have a flatter structure. By flatter, I mean that there is not a strong sense of hierarchy within the index, of metatopic, supermain, and regular discussions. Instead, as seen above, only certain types of detail are picked up, and some detail is gathered and double-posted, where appropriate, as in the North Shore array. Nor are there a lot of interrelationships that need to be reflected through subheadings or cross-references. In this sense, guidebook indexes are simpler, more like a list, so long as what to include is clearly defined and the index meets the audience's needs.

CHILDREN'S BOOKS

Children deserve indexes too. The catch is that children are often new to or still learning how indexes work, and so the index should be designed to be as easy to use as possible.

Children's books encompass a wide range of ages and reading and comprehension abilities. Make sure that the index is age appropriate and matches how the book is written, in terms of length, complexity, and term selection.

If there is space, consider beginning the index with a headnote, perhaps a paragraph in length, explaining how to use the index. Use age-appropriate language.

For the index itself, use indented format, which is easier to scan. The font size and layout should also facilitate navigation.

When selecting terms, stick to significant, concrete discussions. Avoid passing mentions. When readers go to the page that they are directed to, the relevant information should be obvious.

Keep in mind that children are still learning vocabulary and how language works, which can make it challenging to predict which terms the readers will use to search. Brainstorm likely synonyms and provide lots of access points. If possible, double-post instead of using cross-references, so that the children have one less step to finding what they want.

Arrays should also be simple. Limit subheadings, which may confuse children, while also avoiding long strings of locators, which can be intimidating to search. On the other hand, it may be appropriate to gather and double-post entries under a few big-picture categories, such as all of the animals under "animals."

For more information, the Society of Indexers, in the United Kingdom, has published *Indexing Children's Books*, by K.G.B. Bakewell and Paula L. Williams, which I have found quite helpful.

COOKBOOKS

Many indexers enjoy and specialize in indexing cookbooks. A thorough and well-organized index is vital for readers wanting to quickly find a specific recipe. Cookbooks can also be notorious for having limited space for the index, which can provide a good exercise for determining what is truly important to include and how to creatively squeeze in more entries.

The first task is to determine what is indexable. Recipe titles should be indexed, of course. Ingredients should also be indexed, though not all ingredients are of equal value. Differentiate between staple and feature ingredients, with the index focused on what makes the dish stand out. For example, in a bread book, white flour is probably not indexable as it will appear in most recipes, but specialty flours, like almond or buckwheat, are indexable. Some ingredients may also be both a staple and a feature, depending on the context. For example, eggs may be a staple in baking and a feature in eggs pomodoro.

For recipe titles, pay attention to how titles are phrased and how readers may search. Focus on the meat of the title and consider inverting titles that begin with a word or phrase that readers are less likely to remember. For example, "Uncle Jim's Jumbo Baked Beans" and "Crazy Tofu Scramble" may be better indexed as "Baked Beans, Uncle Jim's Jumbo" and "Tofu Scramble, Crazy."

If there is space, gather and double-post recipes under broad arrays, such as desserts, salads, and soups, for readers looking for a quick overview.

Alternatively, to save space, do not double-post recipes if the title and the feature ingredient sort next to each other. Instead, just index as subheadings under the ingredient. For example,

>   Apple and Peach Cobbler
>   Apple Tea
>   Apple Pie, Scrumptious
>   apples
>   Apple and Peach Cobbler
>   Apple Tea
>   Braised Leeks and Apples
>   Candied Apples
>   German Baked Apples
>   Scrumptious Apple Pie
>   Apples, Candied

can simply be

>   apples
>   Apple and Peach Cobbler
>   Apple Tea
>   Braised Leeks and Apples
>   Candied Apples
>   German Baked Apples
>   Scrumptious Apple Pie

For more tips, Thérèse Shere has an excellent article, "Indexing Recipe Titles," which is available on her website. Gillian Watts has also written two wonderful articles, published in *The Indexer*: "Food for thought: the expanding universe of cookbook indexing" (vol. 32, no. 4) and "More food for thought: grains and granularity in cookbook indexing," (vol. 36, no. 4).

HEALTH AND MEDICAL BOOKS

Though related, health books are written for a general audience, while medical books are intended for medical professionals. The indexes required for each can be quite different.

Health books aim to help readers make informed decisions, whether about preventive measures, advice for living with a particular disease, or how to support others through an illness or health episode. Though often written by health professionals, health books are written in a way that is easy to understand. There may also be an autobiographical component, if the author illustrates using their own experience. Health books fall within the trade book category.

Given its lay audience, as well as its intended use as a resource, indexes for health books should be thorough. When selecting terms, include medical terms used in the book as well as entries written in plain language, for readers unfamiliar with medical terminology. I also once received instructions from a client to index all mentions of diseases and symptoms. The rationale was that potential readers may be more likely to buy the book if, while browsing, they were able to find their own symptoms in the index. A bit grim, and also a good reminder that the index can be a marketing tool.

Medical books, on the other hand, assume that readers already have a certain level of expertise. Ideally, indexers should also have some grounding in health and medicine, especially terminology. Use the specialized medical terminology, with cross-references from alternative terms. The index should include a lot of detail and be structured for easy navigation, as the index is likely to be the primary access point to the text and users will want to find answers quickly.

In my own work, I index health books, but not medical books. I do not have a science or healthcare background, and I am not confident that I will properly understand medical texts, or understand how medical professionals think or what medical professionals will need in the index. If you do not have a healthcare background, medical indexing may not be for you either, though it is possible to take courses on medical terminology, if this is an area you want to pursue. For health books, on the other hand, I consider myself part of that lay audience, and health books are written to be accessible. I am much more confident indexing those, and I have indexed several.

For more information, Janyne Ste Marie (now Jayne Rising)'s article "Medical Indexing in the United States," in *The Indexer* (vol. 27, no. 2) provides a brief overview. The book *Indexing Specialties: Medicine*, edited by Pilar Wyman, while at times a bit dated, also provides valuable information.

LEGAL BOOKS

Legal indexing is another area that I do not work in. Legal texts can be significantly larger than trade and scholarly books and very complex. Some understanding of how law works is an asset.

If you are interested to learn more, a good place to start is Kate Mertes' chapter in *Indexing Specialties: Scholarly Books*, edited by Margie Towery and Enid L. Zafran (Information Today, 2005). Also check out *Indexing Specialties: Law*, edited by Peter Kendrick and Enid L. Zafran (Information Today, 2001).

NAME INDEXES

Citations, whether in-text or in the notes, are generally not indexed. The purpose of the index is to point toward discussions, including discussions about people. While acknowledging sources is also important, the place for that is in the notes and bibliography.

The one exception is when a separate names index is required. This is common in a few disciplines, such as psychology. In this scenario, two indexes are written, one composed only of names and the other composed only of concepts and the subject matter.

In the names index, all names, including from the citations, are picked up. Subheadings are not used. Instead of pointing toward discussions, this index is more of a who's who. Undifferentiated locators are acceptable.

The subject index, in contrast, can be written as usual. Index to the hierarchy of information, figure out a good structure, and include subheadings.

If you are not sure whether a names index is required, check with the publisher. If yes, also double-check their expectations for which names to include and how to format. You can also check similar books in the field to see what the convention is.

INDEX LOCORUM AND SCRIPTURE INDEXES

As its name suggests, a scripture index is focused on scripture references, from the Bible or other sacred or ancient sources. Scripture indexes are often found in theological books. An index locorum is a broader term, covering both scripture references and references to classical works, such as Greek and Roman classics.

Similar to name indexes, index locorum pick up all mentions and citations, no matter how brief. It is a tool for finding references, rather than significant discussions. Subheadings, to explain what the references are about, and double-posts are not used.

When picking up references, pick them up exactly as found in the text, even if this means that there are multiple, overlapping entries. In the example below, there is an entry for Revelation 12:7–12, for one discussion, and then separate entries for Revelation 12:9, 12:10, 12:11, and 12:12, which point toward different mentions.

Sorting is also different. Instead of alphabetical sort, sort arrays according to the order of books within the sacred text. For the Bible, use the version that the book you are indexing follows, as different versions arrange the biblical books differently. Other ancient sources can be sorted, roughly speaking, from oldest to new, though check with the publisher for their preference. I also list a few resources below.

Format is important: entries are typically written with the title of the book as the main heading, the chapter and verse as the subheading, followed by the locators. Since the subheading is also composed of numbers—chapter and verse numbers or line numbers—these can be easy to confuse with the locators. Try to find a way to create a visual distinction, such as placing the chapter and verse numbers in bold.

Indented format is easier to scan. However, if there are a lot of references, the index locorum can quickly take up space, and run-in format may be preferred for its efficiency. If space is an issue, play around with the format, including using bold and/or italics for certain elements, to see what is both easy to read and compact.

When indexing scripture references, I often pick these up in a separate pass, either before or after I have drafted the subject index. This helps me to maintain accuracy and thoroughness when picking up the scripture and to avoid losing my train of thought when I am focused on the subject matter.

The following example is from *The Religion of the Apostles*, by Stephen De Young. The scripture index was extensive, and, because the scripture index was cutting into the space available for the subject index, I decided to use run-in format. I also used bold to distinguish the chapter and verses from the locators.

This book also included a few references to extracanonical sources, which is a broad group of books related to the Bible, but usually not considered part of the official canon. There being so few, I decided, after discussing with the publisher, to gather these together at the end of the scripture index. For sorting, I followed the order of deuterocanonical books, Old Testament pseudepigrapha, and, lastly, a Dead Sea scroll. For the Book of Wisdom and Sirach, I also use a gloss to include their alternative titles.

To help readers navigate the index, I also included headings for the Old Testament, New Testament, and extracanonical books.

NEW TESTAMENT
...
1 Peter: **1:9,** 209; **1:10-12,** 46; **1:18-19,** 181, 186; **1:19,** 209; **2:9-12,** 264; **3:18,** 60; **3:18-20,** 87;
2 Peter: **1:1-2,** 46; **1:3-10,** 230; **1:16-18,** 7, 46; **1:21,** 46, 56; **2:4,** 70, 77, 106
1 John: **1-2,** 7; **1:7,** 181, 221; **1:9,** 220; **2:2,** 192–93; **2:22-24,** 46; **3:2,** 83; **3:8,** 107, 194, 197; **3:12-13,** 194; **4:2,** 33; **5:19,** 107, 194, 197; **5:20-21,** 47
2 John: **9,** 47
Jude: **5,** 18, 46; **6,** 70; **6-7,** 106–7; **7-8,** 31; **9,** 115, 124, 185; **25,** 187
Revelation: **1:5,** 181, 209; **1:8,** 49; **1:13,** 29; **1:17,** 49; **1:17-18,** 48; **1:20,** 80, 82; **2:13,** 77; **4,** 48; **4:4,** 129; **4:8-9,** 49; **4:9-11,** 139; **4:10,** 129; **5:1-9,** 48; **5:5-14,** 129; **5:6,** 186, 209; **5:8,** 182; **5:9-12,** 49; **5:13,** 49; **6:9-11,** 139; **6:16,** 49; **7:11-13,** 129; **7:17,** 209; **8:4,** 139; **9:1-3,** 107; **11:1-14,** 124; **11:16,** 129; **12:4,** 129; **12:5,** 117; **12:7,** 117; **12:7-12,** 117; **12:9,** 117; **12:10,** 117; **12:11,** 117, 182; **12:12,** 101; **14:3,** 129; **14:10,** 49, 209; **14:19,** 49; **15:1,** 49; **15:3,** 209; **15:7,** 49; **16:1,** 49; **16:16,** 68; **16:19,** 49; **17:1–18:8,** 258; **19:4,** 129; **19:6,** 209; **19:9,** 209; **19:15,** 49; **20:4-5,** 128; **20:6,** 128, 128n2, 130; **20:10,** 107; **21:1,** 152; **21:5,** 156; **21:6,** 157; **21:22,** 157, 197; **21:23,** 209; **21:25,** 152; **22:1,** 48, 49, 209; **22:3,** 209; **22:8-9,** 48; **22:13-16,** 49

EXTRACANONICAL
1 Maccabees: **12:21,** 208
2 Maccabees: **10:5-8,** 55
Book of Wisdom (Wisdom of Solomon): **4:10-15,** 122
Sirach (Wisdom of Sirach): **44:16,** 122
1 Enoch, 38; **9:6,** 107; **10:8,** 107, 194; **15:8-9,** 111; **21:6-7,** 106; **48:2-10,** 28
Book of Jubilees: **10:8,** 112
Testament of Dan: **6:1-2,** 116n7
4QDeuteronomy, 71

If you are interested in learning more, Potomac Indexing has put together a helpful PDF, available for free on their website. Kate Mertes also has a webinar on index locorum, hosted by the American Society for Indexing. *The SBL Handbook of Style* is also an excellent resource for biblical and ancient sources.

FICTION AND FICTIONAL CHARACTERS

I suspect that most indexers, at some point in their career, fantasize about indexing fiction. Many of us enjoy reading fiction, and it can be an interesting thought experiment to consider how indexes, which are almost exclusively used for nonfiction, can be adapted.

There are a handful of prominent examples of indexes for fictional works, yet in my experience, fiction publishers do not hire indexers. Still, here are a few thoughts on how indexes for fiction might come together. Also, even if fiction itself it not indexed, fictional characters can appear in nonfiction, such as literary criticism.

Of the indexes for fiction that I am aware of, my favorite is for the novel *The Life of My Mother*, by Oskar Maria Graf. As Florian Ehrensperger discusses in *The Indexer*, *The Life of My Mother* is a German novel about Bavarian peasant life in the late 1800s and early 1900s. Because the novel is written so realistically, it can now be used as a resource for historical research. Ten separate indexes have been written, for "personal names, professions, places, animals, plants, food, praying, clothes, technical innovations, and a general subject (or 'miscellaneous') index." For me, these indexes highlight that anything and everything in a book is potentially indexable. The question is, is there an audience which is looking for that information? I also find it fascinating that fiction can be snapshots of the times and used to aid our understanding of history, especially the everyday details of life which so often get forgotten.

Another approach is for the author to write an index for their own book, either as part of the novel itself or as a playful extension. Two examples of this are *Pale Fire*, by Vladimir Nabokov, and *Sylvie and Bruno*, by Lewis Carroll.

When indexing fiction, first decide what the purpose is of the index. This also ties into the intended audience. Is the index part of the story or a tool to access the story? Is the index for scholars or for fans? Will the index be serious, playful, or both? What is it about the story that needs to be revealed though the index?

Next, how much of the narrative should be revealed? Are spoilers acceptable? If the purpose of the index is to highlight details about everyday life and culture, for example, then spoilers may not be relevant since the plot itself can be left alone. But if it is important to create arrays for each character, how much of their story arc should be revealed? Should the index tease readers with information? This, again, comes down to audience and the purpose of the index. If the index is for scholarly research, then spoilers may be acceptable and necessary for researchers to quickly find what they want. If for fans and casual readers, then the index can maybe have a little more fun.

Term selection and how headings and subheadings are phrased is also part of how much is revealed. Are subheadings factual and descriptive about what has happened, or ambiguous and non-committal? Or, subheadings can be used sparingly or omitted altogether. This will likely result in long strings of undifferentiated locators, but does avoid giving away the story. The index for *The Lord of the Rings*, by J.R.R. Tolkien is like this. Subheadings are only used to differentiate people within families, and for alternative terms and names or titles, but the actual story is not revealed.

Besides what to include, how to direct readers is also important. What kind of locators should be used? Books are often published in multiple editions and formats. If an index is planned from the start, then an embedded process should be used, as the tags embedded in the text can be used to generate different indexes for different editions. If an index is being written later, after the book has been published, finding universal locators can be much more difficult.

One option may be to use line or paragraph numbers instead of page numbers, though this would require the lines or paragraphs to be marked in each edition, or readers would have to add their own numbers to their copy. A less granular approach is to index to the chapter or section, which is accessible to anyone using any copy. A good example of indexing to the chapter is the online *Encyclopedia WoT*, which contains what is essentially a fan-created index to Robert Jordan's *The Wheel of Time* series.

The *Encyclopedia WoT* is also a good example of differentiating between volumes in a multivolume series. If the index is for a series (in my opinion, many long series could benefit from an index), the locator should also include a volume number or abbreviation, so that readers will know which book to search. The *Encyclopaedia WoT* uses abbreviations. For example, the locator for chapter 1 of the first volume, *The Eye of the World*, is "TEotW,Ch1."

Outside of fiction, fictional characters can pop up in nonfiction. This often happens in literary criticism or film studies, and sometimes in biographies about writers and other creators.

Context is important when determining whether to index fictional characters. If the reference is minor, or if space for the index is limited, then simply indexing the creative work is probably enough. In some cases, though, the characters themselves are extensively discussed, and should be included as an indexable subject.

A key question, when indexing fictional names, is whether to invert the first and last name. The convention for Western names is to invert, but fictional names exist more in the popular imagination than in official records. Think about how the character is commonly known and look to see how the author handles the name in the text. Some characters, like Bambi or Alice, from *Alice's Adventures in Wonderland*, only have a single name. Other characters, like Oliver Twist or Peter Pan, are either known by the first name or their whole name is treated as a single unit. While yet others, like Mr. Darcy or Jean-Luc Picard, are well-known by their surname. To accommodate all readers, the best option, if there is space, may be to choose a preferred format and include a cross-reference from the alternative. I also suggest being consistent for all fictional names in the index.

It is also a good idea to include a gloss, to differentiate fictional characters from the names of real people. This can be a generic gloss for all characters in the index, or it can be the name of the creative work. For example,

Baggins, Frodo, in *Lord of the Rings*
Luke Skywalker (*Star Wars*)
Maisel, Miriam "Midge" (fictional character)
Pluto (Disney character)

POLICIES AND PROCEDURES, REPORTS, AND USER MANUALS

While this book has focused on indexing books, other documents can be indexed too. This includes policies and procedures, reports, and user manuals. These documents can be either for internal use within an organization or be publicly available. Documents can also be of any length; there is no minimum page requirement. The deciding factor should be whether there is an audience that will benefit from using the index. Even if that is just an audience of one, allowing that person to perform their job better and more efficiently is worthwhile.

Policies and procedures can be surprisingly work intensive to index, even if the document itself is short. Instead of chapters and paragraphs with a narrative flow, sections of the document can be written as a bulleted or numbered list, with each point addressing a specific issue. In my experience, there can easily be ten or more policies per page. If each policy produces, on average, at least two entries (taking into account double-posts or multiple elements within a policy that are indexable), then there can quickly be well over twenty entries per page.

The index will also likely become the primary access point for policies and procedures, since most people will not read these documents cover to cover. The index should be very detailed, using lots of subheadings. Clearly differentiate between similar and related subjects to minimize the amount of time that users need to search between multiple locators. Make sure that entries are clearly phrased and provide lots of access points, through double-posts and cross-references. The index will probably be longer than most trade and scholarly indexes, and that is okay. The goal is to provide quick and clear access.

When choosing locators, try to be as granular as possible. If the policies and procedures are numbered with unique identifiers, then use those numbers for the locators instead of page numbers. On a page containing fifteen policies, for example, this will help readers more quickly pinpoint the correct one. Also consider how the document is being published. If as a PDF, page numbers are likely stable and reliable. If as a Word document, look for locators that will retain their relevance even if the document is modified. Do not be afraid to think outside the box. Once, for an internal document, I used the names of employees for locators, as the document outlined all the tasks within that segment of the organization and who was responsible for each. The only criteria for what kind of locator to use is that the index user understands what the locator means and can easily find the relevant information within the document.

Reports and user manuals can be more like indexing a book, in that there is a narrative flow. These can be written and published by governments, corporations, non-profits, or non-governmental organizations, for either internal or external use. Because reports may be short, the index may also be short, with fewer subheadings needed to break down larger discussions. However, still ensure that all relevant discussions are indexed, including the metatopic and supermain discussions. For locators, page numbers are probably sufficient, unless the document uses section or paragraph numbers, which may be used instead.

TAKEAWAYS

- While the basics of indexing apply to all indexes, different subjects and types of material can have their own specific conventions and requirements.
- Generally speaking, indexes for trade books—written for a general audience—can be a little less detailed and specific, while indexes for scholarly books—usually based on original research and written for

experts or students in the field—should be detailed and comprehensive.

- Indexes for a monograph typically revolve around a single metatopic. Indexes for an edited collection can be thought of as a mash-up of several mini-indexes, with a few arrays to point toward overlapping themes.

- Many resources exist for indexing various subjects and types of books (see page 195). If indexing in a new field, especially for a specialized audience, first do some research so that you are aware of the conventions and expectations.

TRY THIS

Look for books similar to the one that you are indexing. Hopefully, you will find some excellent indexes, but poorly written indexes can also serve as cautionary examples of what to avoid.

What do these other indexes do well? Can you pick up any ideas for how to approach the index structure, term selection, or how the index reflects the contents of the book? What are some things that you may want to avoid or improve upon?

9

Go Forth and Index

WRITING AN INDEX IS A process full of possibility. Each entry represents a decision, made with the reader in mind. Organizing and structuring the index requires care and thought. Seeing the index come together, as an accurate and thorough map of the book, can be immensely satisfying.

Writing an index is also work. As this book describes, there is a lot to keep in mind. Indexing is not a task to be done casually. However, using the lessons and guidance within this book, and following the five-step framework, I believe that writing an excellent index is well within your reach. Now, you just need to put all these lessons into practice.

Make a plan. Read the text. Consider your audience. Peruse other indexes for inspiration. Seek feedback. If you get stuck, consult a resource, whether this book or another.

I believe that you can write an index. You've got this.

BECOMING A PROFESSIONAL INDEXER

If reading this book has inspired or encouraged you to become a professional indexer, or at least sparked your curiosity to learn more, welcome! Building a freelance indexing business also requires a lot of work, and can be a rewarding and long-lasting career.

Most professional indexers run their own, one-person freelancing business. There are occasionally opportunities for indexers to work in-house, for publishers or government, but those opportunities are rare. Many indexers discover the profession later in life as a second or third career and are attracted by the intellectual challenge, the flexibility of being self-employed, and the opportunity to be paid to read widely. Some indexers exclusively index, while others combine indexing with other services, such as editing.

Be aware that it can take a while to market and to start receiving a steady stream of projects. The rule of thumb I've heard is about three years to full-time employment, which matches my experience, though I also know at least one indexer who devised and put into action an extensive marketing campaign and was able to attract full-time work much more quickly. Either way, be aware that it takes time to build a business. It may be best if you also have another source of income in the first few years.

Here are a few things to consider and explore as you move forward.

Practice. The best way to improve as an indexer is to practice. If you do not have a paying project yet, practice writing indexes for books you currently own or for books online in the public domain. Start to build a portfolio—practice indexes count—which you can use to market your services.

Learn. While I believe that this book provides a solid introduction, there is always more to learn. I continue to learn and improve my skills. Formal training, such as courses and webinars, exist, if you are interested in going more in-depth (see page 183). There are also other books and articles (see page 195), especially if there are certain niches that you want to explore.

Network. Indexing can be solitary work. Join an indexing society to connect with other indexers and to access resources (see page 200). Attend indexing conferences. There are also email lists, which are a great place to ask questions and connect with others. Try starting with Indexers' Discussion Group (IDG). For peer reviews, try Index Peer Review.

Business plan. Running a freelance indexing business requires paying attention to the business side of things in addition to indexing. Considerations include marketing, invoicing, taxes, business name and structure, and an office and equipment, whether at home or somewhere else. None of these are insurmountable. All are important to think about.

TRAINING TO BE AN INDEXER

There are several options available for formal training and professional development in indexing, ranging from free and introductory to in-depth instruction. The following list is not exhaustive, and reflects options that I am aware of. You can also check universities and colleges near you to see whether they offer a class.

All these options are available online. Among the indexers I know, the Berkeley course is currently the most popular and comprehensive, though also more expensive. For myself, I took the Simon Fraser University course when I began freelancing, which was a good introduction, though less intensive. The course at the Toronto Metropolitan University (formerly Ryerson University) also provides a good introduction.

- American Society for Indexing (ASI): ASI has its own in-house training program for members, and webinars and two- or three-part online courses available for purchase.
- Indexing Books as a Career: A free MOOC introducing both the indexing process and indexing as a career. Designed by Sylvia Coates, and available from the Canvas Network. www.learn.canvas.net/courses/1332
- Kari Kells, at Index West: For a more personalized approach, indexer Kari Kells offers private lessons. www.karikells.com/Indexer/instruction/
- Simon Fraser University, Indexing: An Essential Art and Science (course)
- Society of Indexers (SI): SI is the indexing society in the United Kingdom, and offers their own in-house training program.
- Toronto Metropolitan University (formerly Ryerson University), Indexing for Books, Journals, and Reports (course)

- University of California Berkeley Extension, Indexing: Theory and Application. The Berkeley course was also developed by Sylvia Coates.

HIRING AN INDEXER

If you are excited to write an index, please skip this section and move on.

I also recognize that indexing is a big task. It may be more work than you anticipated, and you are now looking at the calendar wondering how to make the time, or staring at the page proofs or draft index struggling to make sense of this new way of thinking and organizing. It is also okay if this is you. Indexing is tough. Maybe this particular index is not the right one for you, but at least now you are more prepared for next time, if you want to try again.

If you do decide to hire an indexer, here are a few things to keep in mind and make that process easier.

Give enough time. If you have already started the index and have now changed your mind about writing the index yourself, then you may need to search a little harder to find an available professional. Ideally, start contacting indexers two to three months in advance, or at least a month before the index will be written. Experienced indexers can have their schedules fill up, while newer indexers may be more able to accommodate last-minute queries.

Find an indexer. There are several ways to find an indexer. The publisher may be able to recommend a few. You can also ask colleagues and friends, especially if they have also written books or work in publishing. Most indexing societies also host online directories on their websites, which can be searched by subject matter and other specifications. If the indexer you contact is not available, you can also ask them for recommendations. Depending on how far in advance you ask, it may take several queries before you find someone.

Provide information. When writing to an indexer, provide as much information as you can about the project. This will help the indexer make an informed decision about whether or not the book is a good fit, and will also save time as the indexer will not need to ask so many questions. Include details such as the book's title, the publisher (or mention if you are self-publishing), the subject, and a brief description of the book (or a link to the book's information on the publisher's website). Also include how long the indexable portion of the book is, either word count or page count, as well as the schedule for when the proofs will be ready and when the index will be due. It is okay if all you have at this point are estimates. If you know that an embedded index is needed, also mention that, as not all indexers provide that service.

Ask for information. In addition to providing information, you can also ask your own questions, if you have any. For example, what experience does the indexer have with this subject matter? Can the indexer provide samples, or point toward past books indexed?

Set expectations. This is also the time to set expectations for how you will work with the indexer. For example, do you want to provide input on term selection? Do you want to receive updates on how the index is progressing? Do you want to review the final index and provide feedback? Or do you just want to receive the index at the very end? The indexer may also have expectations and preferences for how this relationship works. While not all indexers enjoy talking on the phone (there is a reason indexing attracts introverts!), a phone or video call may be helpful at this stage, if both parties are comfortable.

Determine costs. Hiring an indexer can be expensive. You are paying for both their time and their expertise. Different indexers approach pricing differently. Some charge based on word count, while others charge based on page count, while yet others charge a flat fee. Some may also charge extra for extensive revisions. As a general rule, indexes for trade books are cheaper than for scholarly books. If you are concerned about cost, you can shop around for a cheaper rate. You may also be able to negotiate a simpler or shorter index for a lower price. For the most part, indexing societies do not publish recommended fees. The Society of Indexers, in the United Kingdom, is the main exception. The American

Society for Indexing publishes executive summaries from their salary surveys, which contains some information about rates. The Indexing Society of Canada also provides information about the various factors that go into pricing.

SOFTWARE FOR INDEXING

Specialized indexing software is useful, but not necessary for writing a good index. The core of indexing is decision making and being consistent in how the index is structured and formatted. All of this can be done manually, though software makes it much easier and faster.

There are currently four main software options. Most professional indexers have their favorite program. The programs all produce indexes that meet professional standards, while having somewhat different functionality. Choosing a program is largely a matter of personal preference. It is worth giving them all a try. Most allow a trial period.

The four programs are:

- Cindex (Windows and Mac)
- Index-Manager (Windows and Mac)
- MACREX (Windows only)
- SKY Index (Windows only)

Full disclosure: I use Cindex, and have not tried the other programs.

Cindex, MACREX, and SKY are designed for traditional back-of-the-book indexing. They are not directly capable of creating embedded indexes, but can work with third-party applications to embed. Index-Manager, in contrast, is specifically designed for an embedded process (see the next section).

Cindex and SKY are available for purchase. Index-Manager is available as a subscription. As of writing, MACREX is currently free, but has limited support.

If you are creating an embedded index, I list additional software options for that in the next section.

If you would like some software assistance, but do not want to learn a completely new program, it is possible to take advantage of indexing capabilities within Word and Excel. For Word, Walter Greulich has published a six-part series in *The Indexer*, starting in the June 2020 issue (vol. 38, no. 2). Greulich is also writing a new series, starting in *The Indexer* June 2022 issue (vol. 40, no. 2), on indexing in Excel.

EBOOK INDEXES AND EMBEDDED INDEXING

Indexes are not only for print books. Ebooks can also contain indexes, with locators that link back to the text, though unfortunately many publishers have not made ebook indexes a priority. The reason I most often hear is that keyword search is an effective replacement (a false assumption), and so linked indexes in ebooks are not necessary. The technology does exist, however, for effective ebook indexes.

The process for creating an ebook index is embedded indexing. This means that tags are inserted into the text—usually either a Word or InDesign document—from which the index is generated. Think of creating and embedding the tags as an additional step, on top of reading the text, creating the entries, and structuring the index.

While the embedding process can be tricky to figure out, there are a few advantages. Page numbers do not need to be final, and the index can be written at an earlier stage, before typesetting. If the text or layout changes, the index is simply regenerated, and can be regenerated as many times as necessary. That said, still plan to index after the book has been edited, as an unedited manuscript can be difficult to work with, and the indexer may have to go back and redo their work if substantial changes are made to the text. Embedded indexes can also be used in multiple formats, both print and electronic. This saves time and money, instead of having to create separate indexes for different formats.

Some publishers require or allow embedded indexes and may even have their own in-house process for you to follow. Before you start indexing, always talk with the publisher first about their requirements, to make sure you are both on the same page.

Word and InDesign both have built-in indexing capabilities. For Word, Walter Greulich explains the process in a series of articles in *The Indexer*, starting in the June 2020 issue (vol. 38, no. 2). However, most professional indexers find indexing in Word or InDesign to be clunky and difficult, and prefer to use third-party programs and plug-ins to make the process easier. A few of the current and common options are listed below. Index-Manager is also a popular standalone indexing program specifically designed for embedded indexes and works with both Word and InDesign files. Keep in mind, however, that most, if not all, of these programs will incur a financial cost, unless you are able to work with a trial version. There will also be the time cost of learning the program. Also remember to check compatibility with your computer operating system. If you would like to first learn more before trying out these programs, many of them have been reviewed in *The Indexer*.

Programs for embedding in Word are:

- DEXembed, from the Editorium (Jack Lyon)
- IndexExploit, from IndexBase (Barry Campbell)
- Index-Manager, from Klarso (Katharina Munk)
- TExtract, from Texzy (Harry Bego)
- WordEmbed, from James Lamb

Programs for embedding in InDesign are:

- Index-Manager, from Klarso (Katharina Munk)
- IndexUtilities, from Kerntiff Publishing Systems

Given the learning curve and probably expense, it may be worth the money to hire a professional to create an embedded index. Another option might be to write the index yourself and then hire someone to create and insert the tags.

Acknowledgments

THIS BOOK ORIGINATED IN A minicourse, Indexing Decoded, which I created in 2019 and was available by email. Other parts of this book draw upon blog posts and reflections that I wrote for my email list. Many thanks to all those who read my reflections, took the minicourse, and sent me feedback and encouragement. It is always a joy to hear that what I have written has been helpful.

My thanks also to Mary Newberry, for her insightful advice and edits to my rough draft, as well as for suggesting the autobiographical index. Also, to Alexandra Peace, for tidying up my writing with her copyedits and her feedback while doing so. And, to Jolanta Komornicka for taking on the index, JoAnne Burek for help with marketing, and David Edelstein for the excellent design. As well, my thanks to Lisa Fedorak, Peter Ullstrom, and Luke Kramer for their feedback on the cover design, and to Lisa Fedorak and Jolanta Komornicka for helping to keep me accountable and on track for the final legs of writing and producing this book. My thanks also to everyone for their forbearance with me as a new and nervous author, and with schedules that didn't go as planned. Producing this book has been quite the ride.

A big thanks is also due to my beta readers, for their encouragement and enthusiasm. I was honestly surprised at how many volunteered their time to read. Their feedback has made this book better. Specifically, my thanks to Samuel Arnet, Jessica McCurdy Crooks, Marianita Dablio,

Lindsay Hobbs, Donald Howes, Amanda Jones, Katie Lewis, Ælfwine Mischler, Shelley Quattrocchi, and Beverly Tyre-Flanagan.

My thanks also to Jennifer Croll and Lara Smith for their encouragement and support.

Last, but not least, many thanks to Elim, my wife, for her love, support, and encouragement as I pursue this dream of being a published author.

Resources

GLOSSARY

Aboutness: Aboutness is a concept which highlights that the text, at all levels of the hierarchy of information, is about something. That aboutness should be reflected in the index.

Array: An array is a complete unit within the index, containing everything the index has to say about a particular subject. This can be as simple and short as a single main heading and locator, or more complex, with a single main heading, multiple subheadings, locators, and cross-references. An array may also be called an entry array, or be used interchangeably with the term entry.

Audience: Audience refers to the people who will be using the index. Keeping these end-users in mind while indexing can help shape which terms are selected and how the index is structured. An index can have multiple audiences, the needs of each the index should anticipate.

Back-of-the-book index: This is an index written for a print book, typically written as a separate document, in contrast to an embedded index.

Cross-references: Cross-references direct readers from one array to another. Cross-references can be one of two types. *See* references redirect readers from a synonym to the preferred term, while *See also* references directs readers to additional and related information.

Double-posting: Double-posting is when the same information is placed in two or more places within the index, for example, as a standalone main entry and as a subheading in relation to a larger context or concept. Or, the same information can be double-posted under synonymous main headings. The wording of the entries can be identically worded or can be tweaked to match the context. The locators for each entry should match.

Em-dash-modified format: This format is an alternative to using sub-subheadings in an array, allowing large arrays to be more easily read.

Embedded index: Tags are created and inserted into the text; the index is later generated from these tags. This allows the index to be written earlier in the book production process, and for the index to be more easily used in multiple formats, including ebooks.

Entry: An entry is the smallest unit in the index, directing readers to a single place in the text or index. An entry may be composed of a main heading and locator, or may include a subheading. A single entry may also form a single array, or multiple entries—all sharing the same main heading—may be combined to form a single, large array. An entry may also be called a record.

Entry array, *see* Array

Explanatory note, *see* Headnote

Force-sorting: The sorting scheme for the index—usually alphabetical sort—is deliberately broken, and an alternative sorting scheme is applied to the main headings and subheadings. This should be done sparingly, and only if it significantly improves usability.

Format: Format refers to the layout of the index, which is how the index appears on the page. The format should facilitate usability. Indexes typically use either indented format or run-in format. Format can also encompass other visual elements, such as whether to abbreviate locators or how to indicate elements such as figures and tables.

Gloss: A parenthetical tag that is sometimes added to a main heading or subheading to provide additional information or context. Also known as a qualifier.

Headnote (explanatory note): A headnote is a brief explanation, usually placed at the beginning of the index, on how to use the index. Headnotes are only necessary if an aspect of the index is particularly complex or unusual; basic and common indexing conventions do not need to be spelled out.

Hierarchy of information: The hierarchy of information is the structure of information within a text, which can be reproduced in the index. The hierarchy begins with the metatopic—what the book as a whole is about—and cascades down through the supermain discussions, regular discussions, and smaller details.

Locator: Locators direct readers to where the information is found. Locators are usually page numbers, but can also be section, paragraph, or policy numbers, so long as the meaning is clear to the reader. Locators can be modified to indicate elements such as footnotes and endnotes, figures and tables, maps and other illustrations, or multiple volumes. Cross-references are also a type of locator. Locators are placed at the end of the entry, following either the main heading or the subheading.

Layout, *see* Format

Main heading: The main heading is the term at the beginning of an array or entry that tells the reader what the array or entry is about. The main heading should be concrete and specific and is usually a noun. Readers should not have to guess the meaning. Main headings can also be called the main entry or simple the heading.

Metatopic: The metatopic is what the whole book, and therefore the index, is about. The metatopic may be simple or be composed of multiple elements, but there is always just one metatopic.

Multiple access points: Providing multiple access points means creating multiple arrays and entries throughout the index through which readers can find the same information. It is a way to anticipate the different ways that readers might search. This allow readers to access information more quickly, and prevents readers from giving up if they cannot immediately find what they are looking for.

Record, *see* Entry

Regular discussions and headings: Regular discussions and headings are smaller discussions that flesh out and support supermain discussions.

Sorting: Sorting refers to how main headings and subheadings are organized in relation to each other. Alphabetical sort is the most common, either letter-by-letter or word-by-word.

Subheading: Subheadings follow the main heading in an entry and provide additional context and information in relation to the main heading. An array can contain multiple subheadings, which break down large discussions into smaller, more digestible chunks, and/or to differentiate between distinct sub-discussions. While one level of subheadings is usually sufficient, multiple levels of subheadings are also possible.

Supermain discussions and headings: Supermain discussions and headings are the discussions which flesh out and support the metatopic.

BOOKS, ARTICLES, AND OTHER RESOURCES

This book is intended as a practical introduction to indexing, covering all the basics. However, there are also many other resources, ranging from introductory to specialized, which you may also find helpful.

General Resources on Indexing

Badgett, Nan. *The Accidental Indexer*. Medford, NJ: Information Today, Inc., 2015.

Browne, Glenda, and Jon Jeremy. *The Indexing Companion*. Cambridge: Cambridge University Press, 2007.

Chicago Manual of Style. 17th ed. Chicago: University of Chicago Press, 2017. (Also available online. The chapter on indexing can also be bought as a standalone volume.)

Duncan, Dennis. *Index, A History of the*. London: Allen Lane, 2021.

Fetters, Linda K. *Handbook of Indexing Techniques: A Guide for Beginning Indexers*. 5th ed. Medford, NJ: Information Today, Inc., 2013

Mulvany, Nancy C. *Indexing Books*. 2nd ed. Chicago: University of Chicago Press, 2005.

National Information Standards Organization (NISO). *ANSI/NISO Z39.4–2021 Criteria for Indexes*. Baltimore: NISO, 2021. DOI: 10.3789/ansi.niso.z39.4–2021.

Perlman, Janet. *Indexing Tactics & Tidbits: An A–Z Guide*. Medford, NJ: Information Today, Inc. with American Society for Indexing, 2016.

Smith, Sherry, and Kari Kells. *Inside Indexing: The Decision-Making Process*. Northwest Indexing Press, 2006.

Stauber, Do Mi. *Facing the Text: Content and Structure in Book Indexing*. Eugene, OR: Cedar Row Press, 2004.

Towery, Margie. *Ten Characteristics of Quality Indexes: Confessions of an Award-Winning Indexer*. Medford, NJ: Information Today, Inc. with American Society for Indexing, 2016.

Wellisch, Hans H. *Indexing from A to Z*. 2nd ed. New York: H. W. Wilson, 1996.

Journals and Newsletters

The Indexer: The International Journal of Indexing is an excellent resource. It contains a wide range of articles, often practical in nature, mostly written by practicing indexers from around the world. The website (www.theindexer.org) contains indexes for searching the journal's contents. While articles less than five years old are behind a paywall, older articles are available for free. You may also be able to gain online access through your local library.

The American Society for Indexing also publishes a journal, *Key Words*, which is available to members or may also be accessible through your library. Some of the other indexing societies also publish newsletters, which are generally for members only.

Biographies and Names

Bell, Hazel K. "Biographies as soft, narrative texts." *The Indexer* vol. 30, no. 3 (Sept. 2012): 141–146.

Bell, Hazel K. *Indexing Biographies & Other Stories of Human Lives*. 4th ed. Liverpool: University of Liverpool Press, 2020.

Bridge, Noeline, ed. *Indexing Names*. Medford, NJ: Information Today, Inc. with American Society for Indexing, 2012.

Smith, Sherry L. "Name Problems: Dispelling the Simplicity Myth." In *Indexing Names*, edited by Noeline Bridge. Medford, NJ: Information Today, Inc. with American Society for Indexing, 2012.

See also *The Indexer* for articles on names from specific cultures and languages.

Children, Indexing for

Bakewell, K.G.B., and Paula L. Williams. *Indexing Children's Books*. Sheffield: Society of Indexers, 2000.

Williams, Paula L., and K.G.B. Bakewell. "Indexing children's information books." *The Indexer* vol. 21, no. 4 (Oct. 1999): 174–179.

Cookbooks

Nickerson, Alexandra, Fred Leise, and Terri Hudoba, eds. *Indexing Specialties: Cookbooks*. Medford, NJ: Information Today, Inc. with American Society for Indexing, 2009.

Shere, Thérèse. "Indexing Recipe Titles." In *Indexing Specialties: Cookbooks*, edited by Alexandra Nickerson, Fred Leise, and Terri Hudoba. Medford, NJ: Information Today, Inc. with American Society for Indexing, 2009. (Also available on Thérèse Shere's website, shere-indexing.com/Shere_Recipe%20Titles_final.pdf.)

Watts, Gillian. "Food for thought: the expanding universe of cookbook indexing." *The Indexer* vo. 32, no. 4 (Dec. 2014), CP12:1.

Watts, Gillian. "More food for thought: grains and granularity in cookbook indexing," *The Indexer* vol. 36, no. 4 (Dec. 2018), 138–148.

Embedded Indexing

American Society for Indexing. "Digital Trends Task Force." www.asindexing.org/about-indexing/digital-trends-task-force/

Digital Publications Indexing. Special Interest Group, hosted by the American Society for Indexing. www.digital-publications-indexing.org.

Greulich, Walter. "Embedded indexing with Word: new light on an old topic. Part 1: how to monitor creation of an index." *The Indexer* vol. 38, no.2 (June 2020): 207–218.

Greulich, Walter. "Embedded indexing with Word. Part 2—editing entries and making work easier by using macros." *The Indexer* vol. 38, no. 3 (Sept. 2020): 291–306.

Greulich, Walter. "Embedded indexing with Word. Part 3—shifting method and field codes for cross-references and page ranges." *The Indexer* vol. 38, no. 4 (Dec. 2020): 381–398.

Greulich, Walter. "Embedded indexing with Word. Part 4—page reference annotations and functional ebook indexes." *The Indexer* vol. 39, no. 1 (March 2021): 85–100.

Greulich, Walter. "Embedded indexing with Word. Part 5—locators other than page numbers." *The Indexer* vol. 39, no. 2 (June 2021): 183–198.

Greulich, Walter. "Embedded indexing with Word. Part 6—sorting and export of entries." *The Indexer* vol. 39, no. 3 (Sept. 2021): 263–282.

See also *The Indexer* for reviews of specific software as well as new developments, as embedded indexing is an evolving field.

Fiction and Fictional Characters

Bell, Hazel. "Fiction published with indexes: in chronological order of publication." *The Indexer* vol. 25, no. 3 (April 2007): 169–175.

Bell, Hazel. "Indexing fiction: a story of complexity." *The Indexer* vol. 17, no. 4 (Oct. 1991): 251–256.

Bell, Hazel. "Kiss and tell and index." *The Indexer* vol. 21, no. 4 (Oct. 1999): 180–181.

Bell, Hazel. "Thirty-nine to one: indexing the novels of Angela Thirkell." *The Indexer* vol. 21, no. 1 (April 1998): 6–10.

Davis, Madeleine. "Fictional characters in non-fiction works." *The Indexer* vol. 29, no. 2 (June 2011): 65–69.

Duncan, Dennis. "'As if we were reading a good novel': fiction and the index from Richardson to Ballard." *The Indexer* vol. 32, no. 1 (March 2014): 2–11.

Ehrensperger, Florian. "In defence of multiple indexes: or the index as learning tool." *The Indexer* vol. 31, no. 4 (Dec. 2013): 153–158.

Saarti, Jarmo, and Kaisa Hypén. "From Thesaurus to ontology: the development of the Kaunokki Finnish fiction thesaurus." *The Indexer* vol. 28, no. 2 (June 2010): 50–58.

Smith, Sherry L. "Name Problems: Dispelling the Simplicity Myth." In *Indexing Names*, edited by Noeline Bridge. Medford, NJ: Information Today, Inc. with American Society for Indexing, 2012.

Zafran, Enid L. "Names in Fiction." In *Indexing Names*, edited by Noeline Bridge. Medford, NJ: Information Today, Inc. with American Society for Indexing, 2012.

History

Towery, Margie, ed. *Indexing Specialties: History*. Medford, NJ: Information Today, Inc. with American Society for Indexing, 1998.

Trubshaw, Bob. "'A funny lot': indexing and local history books." *The Indexer* vol. 24, no. 4 (Oct. 2005): 184–185.

See also military history, below.

Legal Indexing

Kendrick, Peter, and Enid L. Zafran, eds. *Indexing Specialties: Law*. Medford, NJ: Information Today, Inc. with American Society for Indexing, 2001

Mertes, Kate. "Legal Indexing," in *Indexing Specialties: Scholarly Book*s, edited by Margie Towery and Enid L. Zafran. Medford, NJ: Information Today, Inc. with American Society for Indexing, 2005, 15–30.

Medical Indexing

Ste Marie, Janyne. "Medical Indexing in the United States," *The Indexer* vol. 27, no. 2 (June 2009): 59–61.

Wyman, L. Pilar, ed. *Indexing Specialties: Medicine*. Medford, NJ: Information Today, Inc. with American Society for Indexing, 1999.

Military History

Forder, Michael. "Military indexing: men and machines." *The Indexer* vol. 29, no. 3 (Sept. 2011): C1-C8.

Millis, Kendra H. "Ready, aim, fire: indexing military history." *The Indexer* vol. 36, no. 2 (June 2018): 55–58.

Munro, Richard. "Indexing defence: an indexer's defence." *The Indexer* vol. 24, no. 1 (April 2004): 21–23.

Scripture Indexes and Index Locorum

Andrews, Peter, and Meg Davies. "Notes on the indexing of biblical and related materials." *The Indexer* vol. 26, no. 4 (Dec. 2008): C5:1–6.

Mertes, Kate. "Index Locorum: An Elegant Niche." Webinar. American Society for Indexing, January 15, 2020. www.asindexing.org/webinars/mertes-locorum/

Potomac Indexing. *Scriptures and Ancient Sources: Indexing Best Practices*. 2nd ed. Austin, TX, 2020. www.potomacindexing.com/scripture-and-ancient-sources-indexing/

Society of Biblical Literature. *The SBL Handbook of Style*. 2nd ed. Atlanta, GA: SBL Press, 2014.

Structure and Term Selection

Leise, Fred. "Pan-granularism and specificity." *The Indexer* vol. 34, no. 4 (Dec. 2016): 147–55.

Mertes, Kate. "On aboutness." *The Indexer* vol. 35, no. 2 (June 2017): 77–78.

Mertes, Kate. "Term selection." *The Indexer* vol. 36, no. 2 (June 2018): 48–55.

Towery, Margie. "Metatopic and structure." *The Indexer* vol. 35, no. 2 (June 2017): 72–74.

INDEXING SOCIETIES

There are several indexing societies throughout the world. Most professional indexers belong to at least one. If you are interested in becoming an indexer, joining a society can be an excellent way to join a community and access professional development opportunities. If you are looking to hire an indexer, most societies also host online directories of available indexers.

- American Society for Indexing (ASI)
- Association of Freelance Editors, Proofreaders, and Indexers of Ireland (AFEPI)
- Association of Southern African Indexers and Bibliographers (ASAIB)
- Australian and New Zealand Society of Indexers (ANZSI)
- China Society of Indexers (CSI)
- Deutsches Netzwerk der Indexer (DNI) (Germany)
- Indexing Society of Canada/Société canadienne d'indexation (SCI/SCI)
- Netherlands Indexers Network (NIN)
- Society of Indexers (SI) (UK)

Bibliography of Examples

Allen, S.J. *An Introduction to the Crusades.* Toronto: University of Toronto Press, 2017.

atchison, amy l. *political science is for everybody: an introduction to political science.* Toronto: University of Toronto Press, 2021.

Bird, Kym. *Blowing Up the Skirt of History: Recovered and Reanimated Plays by Early Canadian Women Dramatists, 1876–1920.* Montreal: McGill-Queen's University Press, 2020.

Bradley, Nicholas, ed. *An Echo in the Mountains: Al Purdy After a Century.* Montreal: McGill-Queen's University Press, 2020.

Böhme, Madelaine, Rüdiger Braun, and Florian Breier. *Ancient Bones: Uncovering the Astonishing New Story of How We Became Human.* Translated by Jane Billinghurst. Vancouver: Greystone Books, 2020.

Calkins, Tim. *How to Wash a Chicken: Mastering the Business Presentation.* Vancouver: Page Two Books, 2018.

Cannings, Russell, and Richard Cannings. *Best Places to Bird in British Columbia.* Vancouver: Greystone Books, 2017.

Chambers, Douglas D.C., and David Galbraith. *The Letterbooks of John Evelyn, volumes 1 and 2.* Toronto: University of Toronto Press, 2014.

Davis, Laura K., and Linda M. Morra, eds. *Margaret Laurence and Jack McClelland, Letters.* Edmonton: University of Alberta Press, 2018

De Young, Stephen. *The Religion of the Apostles: Orthodox Christianity in the First Century.* Chesterton, IN: Ancient Faith Publishing, 2021.

Donzelli, Aurora. *One or Two Words: Language and Politics in the Toraja Highlands of Indonesia*. Singapore: NUS Press, 2020.

Dosanjh, Ujjal. *Life After Midnight: India, Canada, and the Road Beyond*. Vancouver: Figure 1 Publishing, 2016.

Gafiuk, Anne. *She Made Them Family: A Wartime Scrapbook from the Prairies*. Calgary: What's in a Story?, 2015.

Gammel, Irene. *I Can Only Paint: The Story of Battlefield Artist Mary Riter Hamilton*. Montreal: McGill-Queen's University Press, 2020.

Granatstein, J.L. *Canada's Army: Waging War and Keeping the Peace*. 3rd ed. Toronto: University of Toronto Press, 2021.

Green, Howard. *Railroader: The Unfiltered Genius and Controversy of Four-Time CEO Hunter Harrison*. Vancouver: Page Two Books, 2018.

Grémillet, David. *The Ocean's Whistleblower: The Remarkable Life and Work of Daniel Pauly*. Translated by Georgia Lyon Froman. Vancouver: Greystone Books, 2021.

Harrington, Jill. *Uncommon Sense: Shift Your Thinking, Take New Action, Boost Your Sales*. Vancouver: Figure 1 Publishing, 2017.

Harrison, Melinda. *Personal Next: What We Can Learn from Elite Athletes Navigating Career Transitions*. Vancouver: LifeTree Media, 2020.

Heck, Kalling. *After Authority: Global Art Cinema and Political Transition*. New Brunswick, NJ: Rutgers University Press, 2020.

Hui, Stephen. *Destination Hikes: In and Around Southwestern British Columbia*. Vancouver: Greystone Books, 2021.

Karras, Alan, and Laura J. Mitchell, eds. *Encounters Old and New in World History: Essays Inspired by Jerry H. Bentley*. Honolulu: University of Hawai'i Press, 2017.

Laczó, Ferenc, ed. *Confronting Devastation: Memoirs of Holocaust Survivors from Hungary*. Toronto: Azrieli Foundation, 2019.

Laurence, Margaret. *Recognition and Revelation: Short Nonfiction Writings*. Edited by Nora Foster Stovel. Montreal: McGill-Queen's University Press, 2020.

McCartney, Leslie, and Gwich'in Tribal Council. *Our Whole Gwich'in Way of Life Has Changed / Gwich'in K'yuu Gwiidandài' Tthak Ejuk Gòonlih: Stories from the People of the Land*. Edmonton: University of Alberta Press, 2021.

O'Brian, John. *The Bomb in the Wilderness: Photography and the Nuclear Era in Canada*. Vancouver: UBC Press, 2020.

Pearce, Fred. *A Trillion Trees: Restoring Our Forests by Trusting in Nature*. Vancouver: Greystone Books, 2021.

Pontefract, Dan. *Open to Think: Slow Down, Think Creatively, and Make Better Decisions*. Vancouver: Figure 1 Publishing, 2018.

Reichwein, PearlAnn, and Karen Wall. *Uplift: Visual Culture at the Banff School of Fine Arts*. Vancouver: UBC Press, 2020.

Ross, W. Gillies. *Hunters on the Track: Willian Penny and the Search for Franklin*. Montreal: McGill-Queen's University Press, 2019.

Roy, Patricia E. *The Collectors: A History of the Royal British Columbia Museum and Archives*. Victoria, BC: Royal British Columbia Museum, 2018.

Savage, Candace. *Strangers in the House: A Prairie Story of Bigotry and Belonging*. Vancouver: Greystone Books, 2019.

Schler, Lynn. *Decolonizing Independence: Statecraft in Nigeria's First Republic and Israeli Interventions*. East Lansing: Michigan State University Press, 2022.

Sivanesan, Haema. *In the Present Moment: Buddhism, Contemporary Art, and Social Practice*. Vancouver: Figure 1 Publishing, 2022.

Smith, Will. *Mountains of Blame: Climate and Culpability in the Philippine Uplands*. Seattle: University of Washington Press, 2020.

Stephen, Scott P. *Masters and Servants: The Hudson's Bay Company and Its North American Workforce, 1668–1786*. Edmonton: University of Alberta Press, 2019.

Todd, Zazie. *Wag: The Science of Making Your Dog Happy*. Vancouver: Greystone Books, 2020.

Triggs, Bruce. *Accordion Revolution: A People's History of the Accordion in North America from the Industrial Revolution to Rock 'n' Roll.* Vancouver: Demian & Sons Publications, 2019.

Waldron, Andrew. *Exploring the Capital: An Architectural Guide to the Ottawa-Gatineau Region.* Vancouver: Figure 1 Publishing, 2017.

Wilson, A.N. *God's Funeral.* New York: W. W. Norton & Company, 1999.

Wohlleben, Peter. *The Hidden Life of Trees: What they Feel, How They Communicate—Discoveries from a Secret World.* Translated by Jane Billinghurst. Vancouver: Greystone Books, 2016.

Index

A

aboutness. *See also* hierarchy of information; metatopic; term selection
   definition, 30, 38
   identifying indexable material and, 36
   letters and journals, 161
   metatopics and, 29, 31
   phrasing and, 132–134
   self-help books, 163
   Try This exercises, 179
Accordion Revolution (Triggs), 127
acronyms, 140–141
After Authority (Heck), 145–146
Allen, S. J.
   An Introduction to the Crusades, 64–65
alphabetization, 81–84, 86, 90, 92. *See also* sorting
Ancient Bones (Böhme, Braun, and Breier), 123–124, 126
ANSI/NISO Z39.4-2021, 123
arrays. *See also* entries; main headings; subheadings
   autobiographical index example, 5, 6
   definition, 5, 16
   indented layout, 64, 69
   purpose of, 25
   run-in layout, 66, 69
   Try This exercises, 26
articles (grammatical), 82–84, 92, 144
atchison, amy l.
   political science is for everybody, 52
audience. *See also* usability
   decisions guided by audience need, 18, 19, 27–29, 36, 38
   determining audience, 28–29, 97
   expectations of, 8
   for fiction indexes, 174
   index comprehensiveness and, 120, 150
   index depth and, 104
   multiple access points for, 58, 60
   scholarly books, 28, 154
   term selection and phrasing, 27–29, 36, 132
   trade books, 28, 154
   Try This exercises, 39, 40
audiovisual materials, 20
author-written indexes, 9–10
autobiographical indexes (author's example), 4–7
   Try This exercises, 13

B

Bell, Hazel
   Indexing Biographies & Other Stories of Human Lives, 86
Best Places to Bird in British Columbia (Cannings and Cannings), 18
best practices. *See* consistency; format; multiple access points; phrasing and wording
biographies and memoirs
   about, 157–158
   em-dash-modified format for, 74–76, 86, 158–159
   glosses in, 140, 159
   index depth and entries per page, 104
   sorting in, 85–86
Bird, Kym
   Blowing Up the Skirt of History, 71
Böhme, Madelaine
   Ancient Bones (with Braun and Breier), 123–124, 126
The Bomb in the Wilderness (O'Brian), 128–130
Bradley, Nicholas
   An Echo in the Mountains, 73–74
Braun, Rüdiger
   Ancient Bones (with Böhme and Brier), 123–124, 126
Breier, Florian
   Ancient Bones (with Böhme and Braun), 123–124, 126
Bridge, Noeline
   Indexing Names, 139
business books, 164
business of indexing, 181–182. *See also* indexers

C

Calkins, Tim
   How to Wash a Chicken, 162–163
Canada's Army (Granatstein), 76–80
Cannings, Richard
   Best Places to Bird in British Columbia (with Russell Cannings), 18
Cannings, Russell
   Best Places to Bird in British Columbia (with Richard Cannings), 18
capitalization, 90, 93
Carroll, Lewis
   Sylvie and Bruno, 174
Chambers, Douglas D. C.
   The Letterbooks of John Evelyn, volumes 1 and 2 (with Galbraith), 122
The Chicago Manual of Style, 12, 20, 21, 63, 69
children's books, 123, 166–167
The Collectors (Roy), 66–67
comprehensiveness, 120–121, 150. *See also* depth of indexing
computer-generated indexes, 2, 101
computer programs for indexing, 101, 107, 186, 188
concordances, 2, 12
Confronting Devastation (Laczó), 136
conjunctions, 17, 82–84, 92
consistency
   in alphabetization, 81, 82
   in format, 63, 93, 126
   key to a good index, 119–120, 150, 186
   space and length and, 150
cookbooks, 28, 104, 147, 167–168
costs, 10. *See also* time
   Try This exercises, 13
creative works, 143–146, 151, 159
cross-references. *See also* double-posting; multiple access points
   associative and hierarchical relationships, 23
   autobiographical index example, 7

for children's books, 167
for creative works, 145–146
definition, 22, 25
double-posting vs, 60
editing of, 24
format, 24
as form of locator, 7
general cross-references, 24, 78
for indented vs run-in indexes, 65, 67
as multiple access points, 58
See and *See also* references, 22–23, 24
from subheadings, 23–24, 78
Try This exercises, 26, 61

D

Davis, Laura K.
   Margaret Laurence and Jack McClelland, Letters (with Morra), 32, 161
Decolonizing Independence (Schler), 54–57
depth of indexing, 104, 121. *See also* comprehensiveness
Destination Hikes (Hui), 165–166
De Young, Stephen
   The Religion of the Apostles, 172–173
diaries and journals, 161–162
Donzelli, Aurora
   One or Two Words, 142
Dosanjh, Ujjal
   Life After Midnight, 74–76
double-posting. *See also* cross-references; multiple access points
   autobiographical index example, 6
   for children's books, 167
   for cookbooks, 168
   for creative works, 144–146, 159
   cross-references vs, 60
   for texts with interweaving elements, 55–57

   index structure and, 43–44
   locators and, 55–57
   multiple access points, 6, 34, 44–46, 59–60
   phrasing adjustments, 55–57

E

ebooks, 187
An Echo in the Mountains (Bradley), 73–74
edited collections vs monographs, 155–156, 179
editing
   for consistency, 120
   cross-references, 24
   framework for, 106–108, 114, 115, 116
   of metatopic array, 109
   proofreading final index, 110, 116
   time management, 11, 98, 106, 115
Ehrensperger, Florian, 174
embedded indexes, 186, 187
em-dash-modified format. *See* format, em-dash-modified
Encounters Old and New in World History (Karras and Mitchell), 155
Encyclopedia WoT, 175–176
endnotes and footnotes, 21, 128–130, 150, 161
entries, 5, 15, 16, 25. *See also* arrays; main headings
   Try This exercises, 26
entry arrays. *See* arrays; entries
explanatory notes, 21, 122–123, 150, 166
Exploring the Capital (Waldron), 9

F

family histories, 157, 159–160
feedback on the index, 108–109, 115, 116
fiction, 174–176

fictional characters, indexing, 176–177
figures, 21, 122
footnotes and endnotes, 21, 128–130, 150, 161
force-sorting, 48, 72, 78, 88–89, 91, 92. *See also* sorting
format, 63–93. *See also* locators; sorting; subheadings
   breaking the rules, 91
   capitalization, 90, 93
   consistency in, 63, 93, 126
   for creative works, 143, 151
   cross-references, 24, 65, 67
   definition, 91
   editing and, 106, 107
   final layout, 109–110
   guidelines for, 63
   headnote placement, 123
   indented vs run-in layout, 64–67, 69, 92, 147, 166
   indexes locorum, 172
   preparation before indexing, 96–97
   punctuation, 65, 66, 67
   space considerations, 64, 66, 92, 147
   sub-subheadings, 67–71, 77–80, 92
   usability, 64, 66, 68–69, 92
   Try This exercises, 93
format, em-dash-modified, 72–80
   about, 72, 81, 92
   for biographies and memoirs, 74–76, 86, 158–159
   bold, use of, 77, 79
   for books about artists and writers, 73–74
   chronological sorting, 86
   for creative works, 145
   force-sorting, 78
   goal of simplicity, 74, 81
   for history books, 76–80
   for scholarly books, 76
   as sub-subheading alternative, 72, 92
   sub-subheadings with, 77–80
   for trade books, 76
framework for indexing, 95–117. *See also* arrays; cross-references; format; locators; phrasing and wording; structure
   about, 95
   assessment and preparation, 96–98, 114, 115
   author's indexing process, 114–115
   drafting the index, 102–106, 114, 116, 157
   editing the index, 106–108, 114, 115, 116
   feedback on the index, 108–109, 115, 116
   lists of terms, indexing from, 110–111, 116
   manuscript preparation, 96
   mark-up, 102, 105, 114
   methods of indexing, 99–101
   proofreading final index, 110, 116
   reading the text, 31, 98, 114, 115
   updating indexes, 112–113, 116
   Try This exercises, 116–117

G

Gafiuk, Anne
   She Made Them Family, 124–125, 127
Galbraith, David
   The Letterbooks of John Evelyn, volumes 1 and 2 (with Chambers), 122
Gammel, Irene
   I Can Only Paint, 158–159
glosses
   about, 139–143, 151
   autobiographical index example, 7
   for creative works, 142, 143

dates in, 146, 159
for fictional characters, 176
generic glosses, 143
relationships marked in, 160
God's Funeral (Wilson), 87–88
Graf, Oskar Maria
The Life of My Mother, 174
Granatstein, J. L.
Canada's Army, 76–80
Green, Howard
Railroader, 32
Grémillet, David
The Ocean's Whistleblower, 86
Greulich, Walter, 187, 188
guidebooks, 28, 164–166
Gwich'in Tribal Council
Our Whole Gwich'in Way of Life Has Changed / Gwich'in K'yuu Gwiidandài' Tthak Ejuk Gòonlih (with McCartney), 29

H

Harrington, Jill
Uncommon Sense, 133–134
Harrison, Melinda
Personal Next, 19
headings. *See* main headings; subheadings
headnotes, 21, 122–123, 150, 166
health books, 169
Heck, Kalling
After Authority, 145–146
The Hidden Life of Trees (Wohlleben), 31
hierarchy of information. *See also* structure
definition, 29–30, 35, 38
depth of indexing, 121
house metaphor, 38
identifying, 31
lists of terms and, 111
main headings, 30

metatopic and, 29
regular discussions, 29, 33–34
significant insignificant details, 30, 35–36
small, specific details, 34–35, 39
supermain discussions, 29, 33
term selection and, 38
Try This exercises, 39
hiring an indexer, 10, 184–185
history books, 76–80, 104, 156–157
how-to books, 41, 162–163
How to Wash a Chicken (Calkins), 162–163
Hui, Stephen
Destination Hikes, 165–166
Hunters on the Track (Ross), 9

I

I Can Only Paint (Gammel), 158–159
illustrations, 21, 122
indexable material
aboutness and, 36
in business books, 164
in cookbooks, 167
creative works, 143–146
footnotes and endnotes, 128–130, 150
frontmatter, 20
in letters and journals indexing, 161
metatopic, 32
multiple indexes and, 9
passing mentions, 30, 36–37
significant insignificant details, 30
Try This exercises, 14
index cards, 99–100
indexers
business considerations, 181–183
hiring, 10, 184–185
software for indexing, 101, 107, 186, 188
training for indexing, 182, 183

indexes
    author-written indexes, 9–10
    basic components, 15–26
    definition, 1, 12
    framework for indexing, 95–117
    as marketing tool, 8, 169
    phrasing and wording, 130–137
    purpose of, 8, 13
    software for indexing, 101, 107, 186, 188
    sorting, 81–90
    structure, 41–62
    term selection, 27–40
indexes locorum, 171–173
Indexing Biographies & Other Stories of Human Lives (Bell), 86
Indexing Books (Mulvany), 90, 99, 104, 105, 147
Indexing Names (Bridge), 139
Indexing Specialties, Law (Kendrick and Zafran), 170
Indexing Specialties, Medicine (Wyman), 170
Indexing Specialties, Scholarly Books (Towery and Zafran), 170
In the Present Moment (Sivanesan), 52
An Introduction to the Crusades (Allen), 64–65

J
jargon, 132, 151, 169
Jordan, Robert
    The Wheel of Time series, 175
journals and letters, 161–162
journals and magazines, 20

K
Karras, Alan
    Encounters Old and New in World History (with Mitchell), 155
Kendrick, Peter
    Indexing Specialties, Law (with Zafran), 170

keyword search, 3, 12, 110–111, 116, 187

L
Laczó, Ferenc
    Confronting Devastation, 136
layout. *See* format
legal indexing, 170
Leise, Fred, 47
length of index. *See* space and length
The Letterbooks of John Evelyn, volumes 1 and 2 (Chambers and Galbraith), 122
letters and journals, 161–162
Life After Midnight (Dosanjh), 74–76
The Life of My Mother (Graf), 174
lists of terms, indexing from, 110–111, 116
locators
    about, 7, 20, 25
    for audiovisual materials, 20
    autobiographical index example, 5, 7
    chapters and sections as, 175, 178
    choosing what to use, 20, 25, 178
    cross-references as form of, 7
    double-posting and, 55–57
    for figures and illustrations, 21, 122
    for footnotes and endnotes, 21, 130
    format and sorting, 20
    for journals and magazines, 20
    line and paragraph numbers as, 175, 178
    for multivolume works, 20
    for policies and procedures documents, 20, 178
    ranges, 20–21, 42
    reflow and, 112
    undifferentiated locators, 19, 91, 123–126, 149, 150, 171
    unruly locators, 126–127, 150
    Try This exercises, 26
The Lord of the Rings (Tolkien), 175

M

magazines and journals, 20
main entries. *See* main headings
main headings. *See also* arrays; entries; subheadings
   about, 16, 25
   articles, conjunctions, and prepositions, 83, 84
   autobiographical index example, 5
   capitalization, 90, 93
   force-sorting, 88–89
   hierarchy of information and, 30
   phrasing, 17, 131, 134
   term selection, 30
   Try This exercises, 26, 93
maps, 21
Margaret Laurence and Jack McClelland, Letters (Davis and Morra), 32, 161
mark-up, 102, 105, 114
Masters and Servants (Stephen), 49–51
McCartney, Leslie
   Our Whole Gwich'in Way of Life Has Changed / Gwich'in K'yuu Gwiidandài' Tthak Ejuk Gòonlih (with Gwich'in Tribal Council), 29
medical books, 104, 147, 169
memoirs. *See* biographies and memoirs
Mertes, Kate, 170, 173
metatopic
   aboutness and, 29, 31
   autobiographical index example, 6
   definition, 6, 29, 31, 39
   editing and, 109
   hierarchy of information and, 29
   house metaphor and, 38
   identifying, 31, 32, 39
   indexability of, 32
   index structure, 42, 49–52, 52–53, 58
   supermain discussions and, 33, 39
   term selection for, 32
   Try This exercises, 39, 40, 61, 62
Mitchell, Laura J.
   Encounters Old and New in World History (with Karras), 155
monographs vs edited collections, 155–156, 179
Morra, Linda M.
   Margaret Laurence and Jack McClelland, Letters (with Davis), 32, 161
Mountains of Blame (Smith), 32, 54
multiple access points. *See also* cross-references; phrasing and wording
   about, 58
   autobiographical index example, 6
   best practices, 58, 61
   children's books, 167
   cross-references as, 58
   double-posting as, 6, 34, 44–46, 59–60
   goal of, 60
   index structure and, 58–60
   space constraints and, 150
   term selection and, 30
   Try This exercises, 61, 62
multiple indexes, 9, 13, 170–173
   Try This exercises, 14
multivolume works, 20
Mulvany, Nancy
   Indexing Books, 90, 99, 104, 105, 147

N

Nabokov, Vladimir
   Pale Fire, 174
name indexes, 9, 170–171
names, 138–139, 139–140, 151, 176
neutral language, 134–136, 151
Newberry, Mary, 35, 122
New Hart's Rules, 21
numbers, 90, 92

O

O'Brian, John
  The Bomb in the Wilderness, 128–130
The Ocean's Whistleblower (Grémillet), 86
offensive language, 137, 151
One or Two Words (Donzelli), 142
Open to Think (Pontefract), 83
Our Whole Gwich'in Way of Life Has Changed / Gwich'in K'yuu Gwiidandài' Tthak Ejuk Gòonlih (McCartney and Gwich'in Tribal Council), 29

P

page numbers. *See* locators
Pale Fire (Nabokov), 174
pan-granularity, 41–47, 61. *See also* structure
passing mentions, 30, 36–37, 39, 91, 149, 166
Pearce, Fred
  A Trillion Trees, 17–18
Personal Next (Harrison), 19
phrasing and wording, 130–137. *See also* term selection
  about, 130
  aboutness and, 132–134
  acronyms, 140–141
  for children's books, 167
  double-posting and adjustments to, 55–57
  format's influence on, 65, 66–67
  glosses, 139–143
  for how-to books, 162–163
  inverting phrases, 131
  jargon and specialized terminology, 132, 151, 169
  main headings, 17, 131, 134
  neutral, unbiased language, 134–136, 151
  offensive language, 137, 151
  plain language, 132–134, 151, 169
  preferred terms, 137
  recipe titles, 167
  subheadings, 6, 17, 66–67, 131, 134–135, 143
  usability, 131–132, 151
policies and procedures documents, 20, 28, 104, 147, 177
political science is for everybody (atchison), 52
Pontefract, Dan
  Open to Think, 83
prepositions, 17, 82–84, 92, 144
process of indexing. *See* framework for indexing
professional indexers. *See* indexers
publishers
  expectations and specifications, 12, 63, 64
  locators and special elements, 21
  space limitations, 148
  sub-subheadings discouraged, 68
  Try This exercises, 93
punctuation, 65, 66, 67

R

Railroader (Green), 32
reading the text, 31, 98, 114, 115
Recognition and Revelation (Stovel), 121
records. *See* entries
reference books, 28, 104, 147
reflow, 112
regular discussions and headings. *See also* supermain discussions and headings
  autobiographical index example, 6
  definition, 39
  hierarchy of information and, 29, 33–34
  house metaphor, 38
  index structure, 43–44, 51
  supermain discussions and, 33, 39

term selection for, 33–34
Try This exercises, 39, 40, 61, 62
Reichwein, PearlAnn
Uplift (with Wall), 33, 34, 36–37
The Religion of the Apostles (De Young), 172–173
reports, 177, 178
Rising, Jayne (Janyne Ste Marie), 170
Ross, W. Gillies
Hunters on the Track, 9
Roy, Patricia
The Collectors, 66–67

S

Savage, Candace
Strangers in the House, 89, 160
The SBL Handbook of Style, 173
Schler, Lynn
Decolonizing Independence, 54–57
scholarly books
about, 154, 178
audience, 28, 154
em-dash-modified format, 76
index depth and entries per page, 104
index length, 147
index structure, 41
subheadings for, 19
term selection, 28
time to index, 11
scripture indexes, 9, 171–173
searching vs indexing, 3, 12, 110–111, 116, 187
See and *See also* references. *See* cross-references
self-help books, 162, 163
She Made Them Family (Gafiuk), 124–125, 127
Shere, Thérèse, 168
significant insignificant details, 30, 35–36, 38, 39
Try This exercises, 40

Sivanesan, Haema
In the Present Moment, 52–53
small, specific details, 34–35, 39, 46–47
Smith, Will
Mountains of Blame, 32, 54
software for indexing, 101, 107, 186, 188
sorting, 81–90
alphabetical sorting, 81–84, 86, 92
articles, conjunctions, and prepositions, 82–84, 92, 144
chronological sorting, 85–86, 88, 92
force-sorting, 48, 72, 78, 88–89, 91, 92
indexes locorum, 171, 172
locators, 20
numbers and symbols, 90, 92, 93
page order sorting, 85, 87–88, 88, 92
titles of works, 144
Try This exercises, 93
space and length
breaking the rules, 91
consistency when working with limits, 150
cookbooks, 167, 168
determining index length, 97, 146–147
general cross-references and, 24
indented vs run-in layout, 64, 66, 92, 147
index comprehensiveness and depth, 104, 121
locators and, 21, 124, 126, 127, 149
multiple access points and, 150
passing mentions and, 149
for scholarly books, 147
for trade books, 147, 154
triage, for space constraints, 147–150, 151, 157
working with space limits, 147–150, 151, 157
Try This exercises, 152

Stauber, Do Mi, 31
Ste Marie, Janyne (Jayne Rising), 170
Stephen, Scott P.
Masters and Servants, 49–51
Stovel, Nora Foster
Recognition and Revelation, 121
Strangers in the House (Savage), 89, 160
structure, 41–62. *See also* hierarchy of information
  about, 41, 61, 91
  assessment before indexing, 97
  difficulty of creating, 6
  double-posting and, 43–44
  editing the index and, 106
  goal of, 49, 58, 61, 81
  guidebooks, 166
  hierarchy of information as starting point, 46, 49, 61
  how-to books, 41
  index depth and entries per page, 104
  interweaving elements in text, 54–57, 58
  letters and journals, 161
  metatopic, 42, 49–51, 52, 52–53, 58
  regular discussions, 43–44, 51
  for scholarly books, 41
  self-help books, 164
  small, specific details within, 46–47
  supermain discussions, 42–43, 51
  table of contents/pan-granular approach, 41–47, 61
  Try This exercises, 61, 62, 179
subentries. *See* subheadings
subheadings. *See also* sorting
  about, 17–19, 25
  articles, conjunctions, and prepositions, 17, 83–84, 144
  autobiographical index example, 5, 6
  capitalization, 91
  cross-references from, 23–24, 24, 78
  in em-dash-modified format, 74
  indented vs run-in layout, 64, 65, 66–67, 68–69
  parallel subheadings, 70
  phrasing of, 6, 17, 66–67, 131, 134–135, 143
  placement, 17
  punctuation, 65, 67
  for scholarly books, 19
  space constraints, 149
  sub-subheadings, 67–71, 77–80, 92
  sub-subheading alternatives, 70, 72, 92
  for trade books, 19
  usability and, 123
  Try This exercises, 26
supermain discussions and headings. *See also* regular discussions and headings
  autobiographical index example, 6
  definition, 29, 33, 39
  hierarchy of information and, 29, 33
  house metaphor and, 38
  index structure, 42–43, 51
  metatopics and, 33, 39
  regular discussions and, 33, 39
  Try This exercises, 39, 40, 61, 62
Sylvie and Bruno (Carroll), 174
symbols, 90, 92, 93

T

tables, 21, 122
tables of contents, 2, 12
technical documentation, 104. *See also* policies and procedures documents
term selection, 27–40. *See also* phrasing and wording
  about, 27
  associative and hierarchical relationships, 23

children's books, 166
definition, 38
for edited collections, 156
for fiction indexes, 175
in good indexes, 30
guided by audience, 27–29, 36, 132
for health books, 169
hierarchy of information and, 31, 38
house metaphor and, 38
main headings, 30
metatopics and, 32
passing mentions, 30, 36–37
preferred terms, 22
reflecting the text, 38
regular discussions, 33–34
for scholarly books, 28
significant insignificant details, 30, 35–36
small, specific details, 34–35
supermain discussions, 33
for trade books, 28
Try This exercises, 179
terms of art, 132, 151, 169
textbooks, 104, 147
time
  for editing the index, 98, 106, 115
  for indexing, 9, 11, 13, 106, 184
  for learning software, 188
  for scholarly books, 11
  time management, 11, 13, 98, 106
  for trade books, 11
  Try This exercises, 13, 117
titles and positions, 139
Todd, Zazie
  Wag, 42–47
Tolkien, J. R. R.
  The Lord of the Rings, 175
Towery, Margie, 33
  Indexing Specialties, Scholarly Books (with Zafran), 170
trade books
  about, 154, 178
  audience, 28, 154

em-dash-modified format, 76
index depth and entries per page, 104
index length, 147, 154
  subheadings for, 19
  term selection, 28
  time to index, 11
training for indexing, 182, 183
translations, 142
Triggs, Bruce
  Accordion Revolution, 127
A Trillion Trees (Pearce), 17–18
typesetting, 109–110, 116

U

unbiased language, 134–136, 151
Uncommon Sense (Harrington), 133–134
updating indexes, 112–113, 116
Uplift (Reichwein and Wall), 33, 34, 36–37
usability. *See also* audience
  broad vs narrow entries, 159
  children's books, 166–167
  consistency, 119–120, 126
  force-sorting, 92
  indented vs run-in layout, 64, 65, 66, 92
  locators, 123–125, 126, 128
  phrasing, 131–132, 151
  subheadings and sub-subheadings, 68–69, 123
  Try This exercises, 93
user manuals, 177, 178

W

Wag (Todd), 42–47
Waldron, Andrew
  Exploring the Capital, 9
Wall, Karen
  Uplift (with Reichwein), 33, 34, 36–37
Watts, Gillian, 168

The Wheel of Time series (Jordan), 175
Wilson, A. N.
  God's Funeral, 87–88
Wohlleben, Peter
  The Hidden Life of Trees, 31
wording. *See* phrasing and wording; term selection
Wyman, Pilar
  Indexing Specialties, Medicine, 170

Z

Zafran, Enid L.
  Indexing Specialties, Law (with Kendrick), 170
  Indexing Specialties, Scholarly Books (with Towery), 170

Thank You

Thank you so much for taking the time to read this book. I hope the lessons contained within have set you on the right track for writing an excellent index.

If you loved this book—or even if love is not the right word—can I ask you a favor? I want this book to find the people who need it, and an honest review at your favorite retailer or a site like Goodreads would go a long way to making that happen. Please consider taking a moment—even right now—to leave a quick review.

If you are interested in learning more about what I am up to, including further reflections on indexing, promotions, and news about future books, please sign up for my newsletter at www.stephenullstrom.com/indexing-newsletter.

About the Author

Stephen Ullstrom is an award-winning indexer who discovered indexing by accident.

While studying political science and creative writing at the University of British Columbia, Stephen joined the Arts Co-op program with the goal of gaining publishing experience. At UBC Press, Stephen was tasked with proofreading indexes, and at Harbour Publishing, Stephen asked if he could try writing one, quickly becoming the in-house indexer.

After working at Harbour for three publishing seasons, Stephen decided to move back to Vancouver and try freelancing. That was in late 2012, and the rest is history.

In 2014, Stephen won the Purple Pen Award, for best new indexer, awarded by the Institute of Certified Indexers for his index for *Strange Visitors: Documents in the History of Indigenous and Settler Relations in Canada from 1876*, edited by Keith D. Smith (University of Toronto Press, 2014). In 2021, Stephen also won the Ewart-Daveluy Award, given by the Indexing Society of Canada/Société canadienne d'indexation (ISC/SCI) for his index for *The Shield of Psalmic Prayer: Reflections on Translating, Interpreting, and Praying the Psalter*, by Donald Sheehan (Ancient Faith Publishing, 2020).

In addition to indexing, Stephen previously served for six years on the executive of the Indexing Society of Canada, and continues to be active in the society. He has also written for *The Indexer* and occasionally speaks at conferences. His favorite subjects to index are Asian studies, religious studies, history, and biography and memoir.

Raised in Taiwan, Stephen currently lives in Edmonton, Alberta, and shares adventures with Elim, his wife.

www.ingramcontent.com/pod-product-compliance
Lightning Source LLC
Chambersburg PA
CBHW071839230426
43671CB00012B/2002